Daily
Skill Practice

Grade 4

Erin McCarthy

Carson-Dellosa Publishing, LLC
Greensboro, North Carolina

Credits

Content Editor: Jennifer B. Stith
Copy Editor: Sandra Ogle

 Visit *carsondellosa.com* for correlations to Common Core State, national, and Canadian provincial standards.

Carson-Dellosa Publishing, LLC
PO Box 35665
Greensboro, NC 27425 USA
carsondellosa.com

ISBN 978-1-62442-602-5

04-252131151

Table of Contents

Introduction 4

Incorporating the Standards for
Mathematical Practice 5

Common Core State Standards
Alignment Matrix 7

Week 1 9

Week 2 11

Week 3 13

Week 4 15

Week 5 17

Week 6 19

Week 7 21

Week 8 23

Week 9 25

Week 10 27

Week 11 29

Week 12 31

Week 13 33

Week 14 35

Week 15 37

Week 16 39

Week 17 41

Week 18 43

Week 19 45

Week 20 47

Week 21 49

Week 22 51

Week 23 53

Week 24 55

Week 25 57

Week 26 59

Week 27 61

Week 28 63

Week 29 65

Week 30 67

Week 31 69

Week 32 71

Week 33 73

Week 34 75

Week 35 77

Week 36 79

Week 37 81

Week 38 83

Week 39 85

Week 40 87

Answer Key 89

Common Core Math 4 Today: Daily Skill Practice is a perfect supplement to any classroom math curriculum. Students' math skills will grow as they work on numbers, operations, algebraic thinking, place value, measurement, data, and geometry.

This book covers 40 weeks of daily practice. Four math problems a day for four days a week will provide students with ample practice in math skills. A separate assessment of 10 questions is included for the fifth day of each week.

Various skills and concepts are reinforced throughout the book through activities that align to the Common Core State Standards. To view these standards, please see the Common Core State Standards Alignment Matrix on pages 7 and 8.

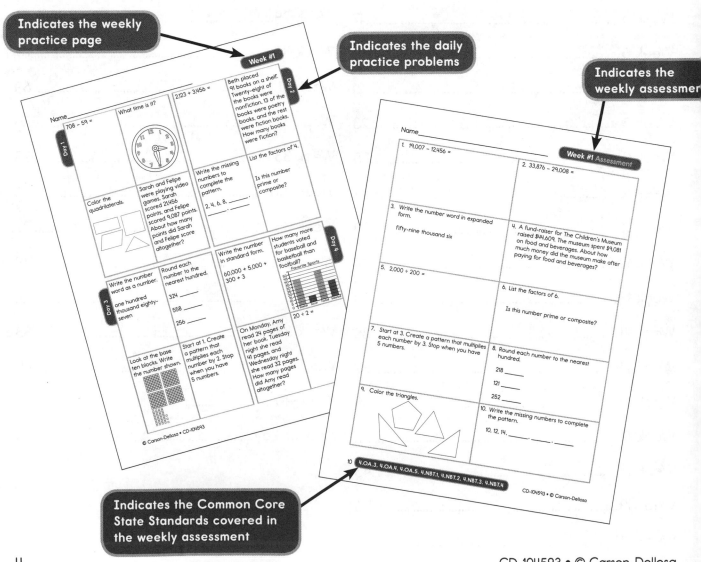

Indicates the weekly practice page

Indicates the daily practice problems

Indicates the weekly assessment

Indicates the Common Core State Standards covered in the weekly assessment

Incorporating the Standards for Mathematical Practice

The daily practice problems and weekly assessments in *Common Core Math 4 Today: Daily Skill Practice* help students achieve proficiency with the grade-level Common Core State Standards. Throughout the year, students should also work on building their comfort with the Standards for Mathematical Practice. Use the following suggestions to extend the problems in *Common Core Math 4 Today: Daily Skill Practice*.

1. **Make sense of problems and persevere in solving them.**

   Students should make sure that they understand a problem before trying to solve it. After solving, students should check their answers, often just by asking themselves if their answers make sense in the context of the question. Incorporate the following ideas into your Math 4 Today time:

   • Encourage students to underline the important parts of word problems and to draw lines through any extra information.
   • Allow students to talk through their answers with partners and explain why they think their answers make sense.

2. **Reason abstractly and quantitatively.**

   Students should be able to represent problems with numbers and symbols without losing the original meaning of the numbers and the symbols. A student who is successful at this practice will be able to reason about questions related to the original problem and use flexibility in solving problems. Incorporate the following ideas into your Math 4 Today time:

   • Ask students questions to extend the problems. For example, if a problem asks students to evenly divide a set of 10, ask them to describe what they would do if the set increased to 11.
   • Have students choose a computation problem and write a word problem to accompany it.

3. **Construct viable arguments and critique the reasoning of others.**

   Students should understand mathematical concepts well enough to be able to reason about and prove or disprove answers. As students become more comfortable with mathematical language, they should use math talk to explain their thinking. Incorporate the following ideas into your Math 4 Today time:

   • Have students work with partners and use mathematical language to explain their ways of thinking about a problem.
   • Encourage students to use manipulatives and drawings to support their reasoning.

4. **Model with mathematics.**

   Students should apply their mathematical knowledge to situations in the real world. They can use drawings, graphs, charts, and other tools to make sense of situations, as well as use skills such as estimation to approach a problem before solving it. Incorporate the following ideas into your Math 4 Today time:

Incorporating the Standards for Mathematical Practice

- Encourage students to take a problem they have solved and explain how it could help them solve a problem in their own lives.
- Ask students to identify tools, such as charts or graphs, that could help them solve a problem.

5. **Use appropriate tools strategically.**

   Students should be able to use a range of tools to help them solve problems, as well as make decisions about which tools to use in different situations. Proficient students will use skills such as estimation to evaluate if the tools helped them solve the problem correctly. Incorporate the following ideas into your Math 4 Today time:

   - Ask students to discuss which tools would be most and least helpful in solving a problem.
   - As a class, discuss how two students using the same tool could have arrived at the same answer. Encourage students to identify the errors and the limitations in using certain tools.

6. **Attend to precision.**

   Students should be thorough in their use of mathematical symbols and labels. They should understand that without them, and without understanding their meanings, math problems are not as meaningful. Incorporate the following ideas into your Math 4 Today time:

   - Ask students to explain how a problem or an answer would change if a label on a graph were changed.
   - Have students go on a scavenger hunt for the week to identify units of measure in the problems, operations symbols, or graph labels.

7. **Look for and make use of structure.**

   Students identify and use patterns to help them extend their knowledge to new concepts. Understanding patterns and structure will also help students be flexible in their approaches to solving problems. Incorporate the following ideas into your Math 4 Today time:

   - Have students become pattern detectives and look for any patterns in each week's problems.
   - Ask students to substitute a different set of numbers into a problem and see if any patterns emerge.

8. **Look for and express regularity in repeated reasoning.**

   Students are able to use any patterns they notice to find shortcuts that help them solve other problems. They can observe a problem with an eye toward finding repetition, instead of straight computation. Incorporate the following ideas into your Math 4 Today time:

   - Allow students to share any shortcuts they may find during their problem solving. As a class, try to understand why the shortcuts work.
   - When students find patterns, have them explain how the patterns could help them solve other problems.

CD-104593 • © Carson-Dellosa

Common Core State Standards Alignment Matrix

STANDARD	W1	W2	W3	W4	W5	W6	W7	W8	W9	W10	W11	W12	W13	W14	W15	W16	W17	W18	W19	W20
4.OA.1											•	•	•	•	•	•	•	•	•	•
4.OA.2											•	•	•	•	•	•	•	•	•	•
4.OA.3	•										•	•	•	•	•	•	•	•	•	•
4.OA.4	•	•	•	•	•	•	•	•	•	•	•	•			•		•		•	
4.OA.5	•	•	•	•	•	•	•	•	•	•	•		•	•	•	•	•	•	•	
4.NBT.1	•	•	•	•	•	•	•	•	•	•	•					•	•	•	•	•
4.NBT.2	•	•	•	•	•	•	•	•	•	•	•	•	•	•	•	•	•	•	•	•
4.NBT.3	•	•	•	•	•	•	•	•	•	•	•	•	•	•	•	•	•	•	•	•
4.NBT.4	•	•	•	•	•	•	•	•	•	•	•	•	•	•	•	•	•	•	•	•
4.NBT.5			•	•							•	•	•	•	•	•	•	•	•	•
4.NBT.6											•	•	•	•	•	•	•	•	•	•
4.NF.1						•														
4.NF.2																				
4.NF.3a																				
4.NF.3b																				
4.NF.3c																				
4.NF.3d																				
4.NF.4a																				
4.NF.4b																				
4.NF.4c																				
4.NF.5																				
4.NF.6																				
4.NF.7																				
4.MD.1																				
4.MD.2																				
4.MD.3											•	•	•	•	•	•	•	•	•	•
4.MD.4																				
4.MD.5																				
4.MD.6																				
4.MD.7																				
4.G.1																				
4.G.2																				
4.G.3																				

W = Week

STANDARD	W21	W22	W23	W24	W25	W26	W27	W28	W29	W30	W31	W32	W33	W34	W35	W36	W37	W38	W39	W40
4.OA.1	●		●			●		●						●						
4.OA.2	●		●		●		●					●								●
4.OA.3	●		●		●			●	●	●					●					
4.OA.4	●		●			●											●			
4.OA.5	●		●					●	●	●		●		●			●			
4.NBT.1	●		●		●								●						●	
4.NBT.2	●		●		●		●				●			●				●		●
4.NBT.3		●	●		●			●	●	●	●		●	●				●		●
4.NBT.4		●		●	●	●			●		●	●		●	●			●		●
4.NBT.5		●		●	●		●				●	●						●		
4.NBT.6		●					●			●	●			●				●		●
4.NF.1																				
4.NF.2	●	●	●	●	●	●	●	●	●	●						●		●		
4.NF.3a	●	●	●	●	●	●	●	●	●	●		●					●			●
4.NF.3b	●	●	●	●	●	●	●	●	●	●			●					●		
4.NF.3c	●	●	●	●	●	●	●	●	●	●							●	●		
4.NF.3d	●	●	●	●	●	●	●	●	●	●			●				●			●
4.NF.4a						●	●	●	●	●			●				●			
4.NF.4b						●	●	●	●	●				●					●	
4.NF.4c						●	●	●	●	●				●			●			
4.NF.5	●	●	●	●	●	●	●	●	●	●			●				●		●	
4.NF.6	●	●	●	●	●	●	●	●	●	●									●	
4.NF.7						●	●	●	●	●				●						●
4.MD.1											●	●	●	●	●	●	●	●	●	●
4.MD.2											●	●	●	●	●	●	●	●	●	●
4.MD.3		●		●		●														
4.MD.4											●		●				●		●	
4.MD.5													●	●	●					
4.MD.6											●	●	●	●	●	●	●	●	●	●
4.MD.7											●	●	●	●	●	●	●	●	●	●
4.G.1											●	●	●	●	●	●	●	●	●	●
4.G.2											●	●	●	●	●	●	●	●	●	●
4.G.3											●	●	●	●	●	●	●	●	●	●

W = Week

Name_____

Day 1

708 – 59 =

What time is it?

Color the quadrilaterals.

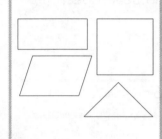

Sarah and Felipe were playing video games. Sarah scored 21,456 points, and Felipe scored 9,087 points. About how many points did Sarah and Felipe score altogether?

Day 2

2,123 + 3,456 =

Beth placed 91 books on a shelf. Twenty-eight of the books were nonfiction, 13 of the books were poetry books, and the rest were fiction books. How many books were fiction?

Write the missing numbers to complete the pattern.

2, 4, 6, 8, _____ , _____ , _____

List the factors of 4.

Is this number prime or composite?

Day 3

Write the number word as a number.

one hundred thousand eighty-seven

Round each number to the nearest hundred.

324 _____

558 _____

256 _____

Look at the base ten blocks. Write the number shown.

Start at 1. Create a pattern that multiplies each number by 2. Stop when you have 5 numbers.

Day 4

Write the number in standard form.

60,000 + 5,000 + 300 + 3

How many more students voted for baseball and basketball than football?

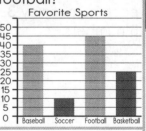

On Monday, Amy read 24 pages of her book. Tuesday night she read 41 pages, and Wednesday night she read 32 pages. How many pages did Amy read altogether?

20 ÷ 2 =

1. 19,007 – 12,456 =	2. 33,876 – 29,008 =
3. Write the number word in expanded form. fifty-nine thousand six	4. A fund-raiser for The Children's Museum raised $44,609. The museum spent $9,081 on food and beverages. About how much money did the museum make after paying for food and beverages?
5. 2,000 ÷ 200 =	6. List the factors of 6. Is this number prime or composite?
7. Start at 3. Create a pattern that multiplies each number by 3. Stop when you have 5 numbers.	8. Round each number to the nearest hundred. 218 _____ 121 _____ 252 _____
9. Color the triangles. 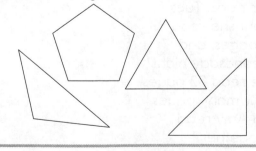	10. Write the missing numbers to complete the pattern. 10, 12, 14, _____, _____, _____

4.OA.3, 4.OA.4, 4.OA.5, 4.NBT.1, 4.NBT.2, 4.NBT.3, 4.NBT.4

Name_____

Day 1

Write the number in standard form.

600,000 + 30,000 + 2,000 + 700 + 70

What units would you use to measure the length of a wall?

A. inches
B. centimeters
C. yards

Day 2

Dawn has to pay $10,990 for her college dorm room and tuition each year. About how much money does Dawn spend the first 2 years of college?

Complete the table.

Add 4	
1	5
3	
8	
16	

The zookeeper takes 2 bags of peanuts to an elephant. Each bag has 12 peanuts. How many peanuts does the zookeeper give to the elephant?

---

400 ÷ 40 =

---

91 + 28 + 13 =

List the factors of 7.

Is this number prime or composite?

Day 3

49,007 – 34,569 =

What time is it?

Day 4

45,678 + 21,456 =

What is the value of the following coins?

2 quarters, 4 dimes, and 6 pennies

---

85 – 31 =

Start at 2. Create a pattern that multiplies each number by 2 and then adds 1. Stop when you have 5 numbers.

What is the name of the figure shown?

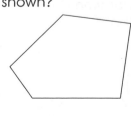

Round 54,878 to the nearest ten thousand.

Name_____

1. Round 43,766 to the nearest thousand.

2. Write the number in standard form.

   four hundred thousand two

3. 30,000 ÷ 3,000 =

4. List the factors of 10.

   Is this number prime or composite?

5. Start at 5. Create a pattern that adds 3 to each number. Stop when you have 5 numbers.

6. $1,358 + $7,649 =

7. 17,456 – 7,656 =

8. Complete the table.

Add 10	
41	51
57	
47	
52	

9. Austin has to be at school by the time shown on the clock. What time does Austin have to be at school?

10. What is the name of the figure shown?

4.OA.4, 4.OA.5, 4.NBT.1, 4.NBT.2, 4.NBT.3, 4.NBT.4   CD-104593 • © Carson-Dellosa

Name_____

Day 1

Write <, >, or = to make the statement true.

17,987 ◯ 17,877

20 × 5 =

20 × 6 =

20 × 7 =

Round each number to the nearest ten. Then, add.

34 + 81 is about _____.

List the factors of 12.

Is this number prime or composite?

Day 2

Write the number word as a number.

six hundred thousand eight

Write the multiplication sentence shown by the picture.

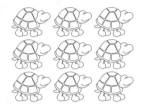

584 + 381 =

Start at 125. Create a pattern that subtracts 6 from each number. Stop when you have 5 numbers.

Day 3

1,102 + 6,206 =

3 × 5 = 15

Write a related multiplication fact.

Addison is reading a book that is 584 pages long. She read 171 pages on Saturday and 207 pages on Sunday. She finished the book on Monday. How many pages did she read on Monday?

500,000 ÷ 50,000 =

Day 4

Round 16,311 to the nearest thousand.

44 + 15 =

82 − 30 =

2 × 9 =

9 × 2 =

8 × 2 =

Write <, >, or = to make the statement true.

626 ◯ 616

Name_____

1. Write <, >, or = to make the statement true.

   973 $\bigcirc$ 937

2. 1,508 + 2,428 =

3. Write the number in standard form.

   50,000 + 1,000 + 200 + 60 + 3

4. Round 45,656 to the nearest hundred.

5. 60 ÷ 6 =

6. Start at 500. Create a pattern that subtracts 4 from each number. Stop when you have 5 numbers.

7. List the factors of 9.

   Is this number prime or composite?

8. 3 × 2 =

   2 × 8 =

   4 × 1 =

9. Write the multiplication sentence shown by the picture.

10. Clay took 73 photos of animals at the zoo. He took 14 photos of monkeys, 21 photos of tigers, and 13 photos of polar bears. How many photos of other animals did Clay take?

Name_____

Day 1

Write the number in standard form.

one million four hundred ninety-six thousand seven hundred seventy-two

4 × _____ = 32

_____ × 9 = 36

2 × 4 = _____

Day 2

Write <, >, or = to make the statement true.

37,000 ◯ 37,607

Gavin is watching 3 spiders crawling on the sidewalk. The fuzzy spider crawls 3 times as far as the brown spider. The brown spider crawls 4 feet. How far does the fuzzy spider crawl?

Choose the related addition sentence for 6 × 3.

A. 6 + 6
B. 3 + 3 + 3 + 3 + 3 + 3
C. 6 + 6 + 6
D. 3 + 3 + 3

Round 183,982 to the nearest ten thousand.

Jessica earned $20 for doing chores. She went to the movies and bought a ticket for $9 and popcorn for $7. How much money does Jessica have left?

700 ÷ 70 =

Day 3

1,747 + 5,844 =

What was the weather mostly like last week?

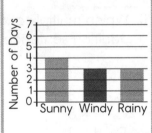

Round each number to the nearest ten. Then, add.

678 + 179 is about _____.

A tree branch has 5 buds. Each day, 2 more buds sprout. How many buds are on the tree branch after the first 5 days? (Hint: Make a T-chart.)

Day 4

2,535 − 2,172 =

5 × 3 = 15

Write a related multiplication fact.

30 × 2 =

30 × 3 =

30 × 4 =

List the factors of 11.

Is this number prime or composite?

1. Write the number in standard form.

   7 ten thousands + 5 thousands + 3 hundreds + 1 ten + 7 ones

2. The tree has 3 acorns under it. Each day, 3 more fall under the tree. How many acorns are under the tree after the first 5 days? (Hint: Make a T-chart.)

3. List the factors of 28.

   Is this number prime or composite?

4. 10,898 + 14,373 =

5. Round 81,294 to the nearest ten.

6. 8,000 ÷ 800 =

7. 1,230 – 954 =

8. Which multiplication fact matches the addition sentence 8 + 8 + 8 + 8?

   A. 2 × 4
   B. 3 × 8
   C. 4 × 8
   D. 8 × 3

9. Hunter earns $3 for each room he cleans in his house. If Hunter cleans 2 rooms and buys a bag of candy for $2, how much money does he have left?

10. 2 × _____ = 10

    _____ × 5 = 25

    4 × 2 = _____

4.OA.4, 4.OA.5, 4.NBT.1, 4.NBT.2, 4.NBT.3, 4.NBT.4, 4.NBT.5

Name_____

Day 1

66,859 − 34,437 =	Write <, >, or = to make the statement true. 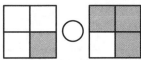

| Write the related multiplication facts.

32 ÷ 4
4 × _____

20 ÷ 5
5 × _____

24 ÷ 6
6 × _____ | Determine the 18th shape in the pattern.  |

Day 2

43,273 + 10,586 =	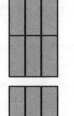 = $\dfrac{}{6}$

| Irene found 11 starfish. Each starfish had 5 arms. How many arms did the starfish have in all? | 900,000 ÷ 90,000 = |

Day 3

| Write the number in standard form.

700,000 + 10,000 + 3,000 + 900 + 20 + 3 | 32 ÷ 8 =

18 ÷ 3 =

5 × 3 = |
|---|---|

| _____ ÷ 3 = 5

20 ÷ _____ = 4

6 × 4 = _____ | Round 567,433 to the nearest hundred thousand. |

Day 4

| Write <, >, or = to make the statement true.

2,414 ◯ 2,419	5 × 2 × 1 =

| Divide this square into eighths. Label each eighth with an appropriate fraction. 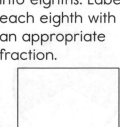 | List the factors of 44.

Is this number prime or composite? |

17

1. List the factors of 35.

   Is this number prime or composite?

2. Determine the 20th shape in the pattern.

3. Write the number in standard form.

   one hundred forty thousand six hundred eighty-seven.

4. Round 87,658 to the nearest thousand.

5. 2,606 + 7,025 =

6. 9,379 − 4,312 =

7. 60,000 ÷ 6,000 =

8. Divide the rectangle into eighths and shade the pieces to show the fraction $\frac{2}{8}$.

9. Write <, >, or = to make the statement true.

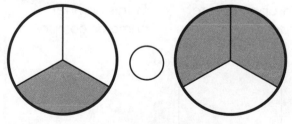

10. 5 × 9 =

    35 ÷ 5 =

    36 ÷ 9 =

Name_____

Day 1

Determine the 17th shape in the pattern.

Quinn runs 3 miles 3 times every week. How many miles does Quinn run in 6 weeks?

Write the number in expanded form.

three hundred thirty-nine thousand six

Round each number to the nearest ten. Then, add.

212 + 87 is about _____.

Day 2

Write <, >, or = to make the statement true.

54,657 ◯ 54,989

$100 \div 10 =$

$40 \times 1 =$

$40 \times 9 =$

$60 \times 1 =$

List the factors of 19.

Is this number prime or composite?

Day 3

$7,678 + $5,444 =

Fill in the missing numbers to complete the pattern.

89, 85, 81, _____, _____, _____

Round 7,667 to the nearest hundred.

Divide the rectangle into sixths. Label each sixth with an appropriate fraction.

Day 4

Are the fractions $\frac{1}{2}$ and $\frac{3}{8}$ equivalent fractions?

Name two fractions on the number line that are equivalent fractions.

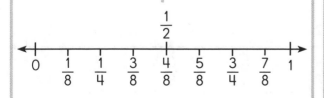

Oliver earns $4 a day for 7 days for doing chores. Each day, his mom takes out $2 and puts it into a savings account for Oliver. How much money does Oliver get to keep after 7 days?

$8,987 − $8,765 =

Name_____

1. 7,495 – 6,816 =	2. Write the number in standard form. 4 ten thousands, 1 thousand, 9 hundreds, 8 tens, and 4 ones
3. 30 ÷ 3 =	4. Round 713,923 to the nearest ten.
5. Determine the 28th shape in the pattern. 	6. List the factors of 30. Is this number prime or composite?
7. 472,936 + 453,250 =	8. 15 ÷ 5 = 56 ÷ 8 = 9 × 8 =

9.

Are the fractions $\frac{1}{2}$ and $\frac{1}{8}$ equivalent fractions?

10.

Are the fractions $\frac{2}{2}$ and $\frac{8}{8}$ equivalent fractions?

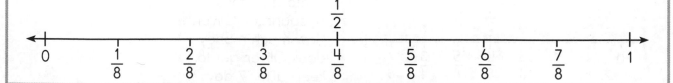

4.OA.4, 4.OA.5, 4.NBT.1, 4.NBT.2, 4.NBT.3, 4.NBT.4, 4.NF.1   CD-104593 • © Carson-Dellosa

Name_____

Day 1

Write the number in standard form.

900,000 + 4,000 + 500 + 3

Are these fractions equivalent fractions?

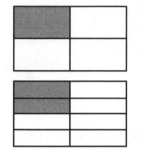

A square has one side that measures 6 inches. What is the perimeter of the square?

5,000 ÷ 500 =

Day 2

7,067 – 4,002 =

Write the fraction.

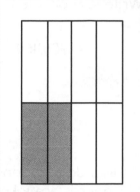

Mia is excited to get to the amusement park. Her family reaches the amusement park at 8:00. They wait in line to get in for 50 minutes. What time do they go in?

Round 34,786 to the nearest ten thousand.

Day 3

16,545 + 24,345 =

---

493 + 327 =

Five spiders are building webs in the barn. How many legs are there in all?

A can has 50 marbles in it. Every hour, 7 marbles are taken out. After 4 hours, how many marbles are left in the can?

Day 4

List the factors of 39.

Is this number prime or composite?

Fill in the missing numbers to complete the pattern.
615, 605, 595,

_____, _____,

_____

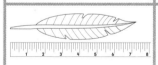

How many inches long is the feather?

Write <, >, or = to make the statement true.

121,453 ◯ 112,678

Name_____

1. Write <, >, or = to make the statement true.

   786,454 ◯ 786,454

2. 234,543 + 344,456 =

3. On Monday, 25 pencils are in a basket. If 3 pencils are taken out of the basket each day, how many pencils are left in the basket on Friday?

4. 90,000 ÷ 9,000 =

5. List the factors of 17.

   Is this number prime or composite?

6. Round 432,115 to the nearest hundred thousand.

7. 27,791 − 13,782 =

8. Write the number in expanded form.

   thirty-eight thousand five hundred twenty-five

9.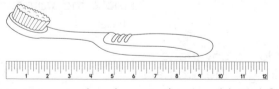

   How many inches long is the toothbrush?

10. The basketball game began at 7:05. The game took 2 hours and 45 minutes to play. What time was the basketball game over?

 CD-104593 • © Carson-Dellosa

Name_____

Day 1

List the factors of 14.

Is this number prime or composite?

Write <, >, or = to make each statement true.

315 ◯ 415

649 ◯ 694

116 ◯ 116

Day 2

Start at 5. Create a pattern that multiplies each number by 3 and subtracts 2. Stop when you have 5 numbers.

Nora places 4 pictures on each of the 5 shelves in her bedroom. How many pictures does Nora place on the shelves in all?

Fill in the missing numbers to complete the pattern.

145, 148, 151,

_____, _____,

_____

Write <, >, or = to make the statement true.

5,874 ◯ 5,784

Color the shapes that have 4 vertices.

Round 95,175 to the nearest thousand.

Day 3

200,000 ÷ 20,000 =

How many more trees were planted in September than November?

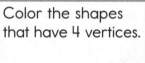

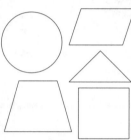

Trees Planted

Sept.	
Oct.	
Nov.	

🌱 = 4 trees

Day 4

Write the number in expanded form.

forty-one thousand nine hundred eighty-four

---

15 + 37 + 10 =

Tomorrow, 567 people will want tickets to a concert. Only 417 tickets are available. How many people will not be able to get tickets?

36,878 + 20,557 =

Write the number in word form.

212

77,528 – 68,431 =

---

1. 214,965 – 104,426 =	2. 452,816 + 240,910 =
3. Round 11,905 to the nearest ten.	4. Write the number in standard form. 60,000 + 6,000 + 400 + 10 + 8
5. 900 ÷ 90 =	6. Start at 4. Create a pattern that multiplies each number by 2 and subtracts 1. Stop when you have 5 numbers.
7. List the factors of 24. Is this number prime or composite?	8. Color the shapes that have 4 sides.
9. How many more students have dogs and cats than fish and birds?	10. Fill in the missing numbers to complete the pattern. 203, 206, 209, _____, _____, _____

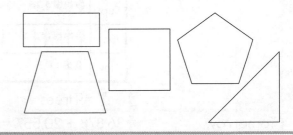

Students' Pets

Dog	🐾🐾🐾🐾🐾🐾
Cat	🐾🐾🐾🐾🐾
Fish	🐾🐾🐾🐾
Bird	🐾🐾

🐾 = 3 students

Name_____

Day 1

543,786 + 89,009 =	18 ÷ _____ = 2 _____ ÷ 6 = 7 36 ÷ 4 = _____
847 − 358 =	List the factors of 36. Is this number prime or composite?

Day 2

78,908 − 40,000 =	Round to the nearest ten. Then, subtract. 453 − 110 is about _____.
Mr. Garcia buys 48 flowers. He puts 6 flowers in each vase. If he sells each vase for $2, how much money does he earn?	Determine the 11th shape in the pattern. △ ○ ■ ●

Day 3

Write <, >, or = to make the statement true. 87,877 ◯ 877,505	70 × 5 = 70 × 3 = 50 × 9 =
Write a related multiplication fact for the following division sentence. 54 ÷ 6 = 9	400,000 ÷ 40,000 =

Day 4

Write the number word as a number. ninety-five thousand one hundred seventy-five	Leo has 24 golf clubs. He has 3 golf bags. Each bag contains the same number of clubs. How many golf clubs are in each bag?
Show how to solve this problem. 5 × 5 × 4 =	Last year, Langdon School had $127,657 available for scholarships. This year, the school has $141,509 available. About how much more money does the school have for scholarships this year?

Name_____

1. Ella earned $435 in June and $543 in July. About how much money in all did Ella earn in June and July?

2. Determine the 25th shape in the pattern.

3. 70 ÷ 7 =

4. List the factors of 23.

   Is this number prime or composite?

5. Write the number in expanded form.

   2,124

6. Write <, >, or = to make the statement true.

   3,864 ◯ 3,864

7. 14,543 – 13,999 =

8. 506,291 + 112,867 =

9. _____ × 6 = 18

   7 × _____ = 42

   8 × 2 = _____

10. Kaylen has 15 golf balls to put into buckets. She puts 5 golf balls into each bucket. How many buckets did Kaylen use?

Name_____

Day 1

Round 921,444 to the nearest hundred thousand.

Pedro parks his car at 4:03. He wants to visit the bookstore, so he puts enough money in the parking meter for one hour. What time should he be back at his car?

476 + 498 =

On the day she was born, a baby leopard had 9 spots. Each day, 4 more spots appeared. After 5 days, how many spots did the baby leopard have? (Hint: Make a T-chart.)

Day 2

493,422 + 292,434 =

An average-sized dog weighs about

A. 15 grams.
B. 50 grams.
C. 5,000 grams.
D. 15,000 grams.

4 × 2 =

6 ÷ 3 =

14 ÷ 7 =

Write the number in standard form.

80,000 + 7,000 + 400 + 70 + 8

Day 3

87,223 – 8,224 =

Draw square units to show the area of the rectangle.

4

7

Write <, >, or = to make the statement true.

$\frac{1}{8}$ ◯ $\frac{5}{8}$

Write <, >, or = to make the statement true.

502,142 ◯ 502,442

Day 4

List the factors of 20.

Is this number prime or composite?

What is the perimeter of the shape?

1 cm   6 cm

4 cm   4 cm

3 cm   2 cm

Are these fractions equivalent fractions? Circle *yes* or *no*.

yes   no

10,000 ÷ 1,000 =

1. $800,000 \div 80,000 =$	2. List the factors of 33. Is this number prime or composite?
3. $87,602 - 59,899 =$	4. $14,543 + 41,208 =$
5. Brian has 40 stickers. He shares 5 stickers with his friends every day. After 5 days, how many stickers will Brian have left? (Hint: Make a T-chart.)	6. Round 16,567 to the nearest thousand.
7. Write the number in expanded form. 259,341	8. Write <, >, or = to make the statement true. 307,199 ◯ 370,199
9. Draw square units to show the area of the rectangle. 2 ⬜ 4	10. A nail weighs about A. 1 gram. B. 10 grams. C. 100 grams. D. 1,000 grams.

4.OA.4, 4.OA.5, 4.NBT.1, 4.NBT.2, 4.NBT.3, 4.NBT.4

Day 1

Write the equation.

Reid is 3 years old. His sister is 4 times older. How old is Reid's sister?

Round 26,127 to the nearest hundred.

Chelsea's family traveled 300 miles by car each day during their family vacation. How many miles did Chelsea's family travel over all 6 days?

Start at 10. Create a pattern that multiplies each number by 10. Stop when you have 5 numbers.

Day 2

Write <, >, or = to make the statement true.

642,199 $\bigcirc$ 624,199

$70 \times 3 =$

$78,644 + 43,987 =$

Find the perimeter.

1 cm

2 cm

Day 3

Paige saw 142 tourists in July, August, and September. She saw 32 tourists in July and 89 tourists in August. How many tourists did Paige see in September?

List the factors of 79.

Is this number prime or composite?

$21 \div 3 =$

$24 \div 6 =$

$50 \div 10 =$

$4,000 \div 400 =$

Day 4

$97,808 - 31,876 =$

Find the area.

10 m

7 m

Write the number word as a number.

thirty-seven thousand eight hundred ninety

$40 \times 2 =$

1. Rachel filled all 15 shelves in her room with books. She placed 9 books on each shelf. How many books did she place on all 15 shelves?

2. $80 \times 4 =$

3. Round 639,121 to the nearest ten thousand.

4. Find the perimeter.

1 ft.

3 ft.

5. Start at 5. Create a pattern that multiplies each number by 5. Stop when you have 5 numbers.

6. Write the equation.

Tia has 7 hair bows. Her sister has 6 times as many as Tia. How many hair bows does Tia's sister have?

7. $72 \div 9 =$

$77 \div 11 =$

$144 \div 12 =$

8. List the factors of 84.

Is this number prime or composite?

9. Find the area.

1 m

20 m

10. Mario took 57 photos of landmarks in the city he visited. He took 12 photos of buildings, 16 photos of bridges, and 2 photos of statues. The rest were photos of parks. How many photos of parks did Mario take?

Day 1

A swimming pool has a perimeter of 72 feet. The short sides measure 16 feet. What is the length of the longer sides of the pool?

Write the number in standard form.

800,000 + 20,000 + 7,000 + 600 + 70 + 7

Day 2

Write the equation.

Jay mows 1 lawn every day Monday through Saturday. He is paid $25 for each lawn. How much money does Jay earn mowing lawns?

$70,000 \div 7,000 =$

$38 \times 7 =$

Sixty-four students voted for Morgan. Two times as many students voted for Whitney. How many students voted altogether?

List the factors of 60.

Is this number prime or composite?

$82 \times 5 =$

Day 3

A total of 100 fourth graders are being divided equally between 5 fourth-grade teachers. How many students will be in each class?

$73,856 + 51,313 =$

Day 4

The area of a window measures 336 square inches. If the window is 16 inches wide, how long is the window?

$73,461 - 3,861 =$

$66 \times 8 =$

$56 \div 8 =$

$11 \div 11 =$

$16 \div 8 =$

Round 438,692 to the nearest thousand.

$41 \times 6 =$

---

1. $97 \times 4 =$

2. Twenty-two people voted for fish as their favorite pet. Three times as many people voted for dogs. How many people voted in all?

3. Write the equation.

   Macon eats 33 animal crackers as a snack every day after school. How many animal crackers does she eat during a 5-day school week?

4. $36 \div 12 =$

   $16 \div 8 =$

   $64 \div 8 =$

5. $67 \times 9 =$

6. A rectangular blanket's perimeter is 210 inches. If the long sides of the blanket measure 60 inches, what is the length of the shorter sides of the blanket?

7. The door to the clubhouse has an area of 1,792 square centimeters. If the length of the door is 56 centimeters, how wide is the door?

8. Write the number in expanded form.

   87,478

9. $600 \div 60 =$

10. The town hall's bells ring 8 times every hour. How many times do the bells ring in a 24-hour period?

Day 1

$837 \div 9 =$

Matthew unpacked 43 boxes of lightbulbs for the discount warehouse. Each box contained 6 bulbs. How many bulbs were in all 43 boxes?

Round 213,548 to the nearest hundred.

The perimeter of a rectangular yard is 204 feet. If the width of the yard is 45 feet, what is the length of the yard?

Day 2

$916 \times 7 =$

Pilar's hair is 7 inches long. If her hair grows 2 inches each month, how long will her hair be after 6 months?

$100,000 \div 10,000 =$

The area of the rectangular roof on a dollhouse is 756 square inches. The length of the roof is 108 inches. How many inches wide is the roof?

Day 3

$232 \times 4 =$

$183,982 + 81,294 =$

Write the number word as a number.

seventeen thousand four hundred thirty-three

Write the equation.

Melanie bought 7 packages of greeting cards. Each package had 9 cards. How many greeting cards did she get in all?

Day 4

$147 \div 3 =$

$7,689 - 6,726 =$

List the factors of 59.

Is this number prime or composite?

Mr. Hamilton gave out 15 coupons per hour at the appliance show. After 2 days at the show, working 14 hours total, how many coupons did he distribute?

1. Molly is 36 inches tall. If she grows 4 inches every year, how tall will she be in 3 years?	2. The perimeter of Raul's picture frame is 108 centimeters. The length of the picture frame is 18 centimeters. What is the width of the picture frame?
3. $184 \div 2 =$	4. $20,893 + 68,352 =$
5. Kelly practiced her flute 30 minutes a day for 9 days. How many total minutes did she practice?	6. Write the equation. Chris walked 4 miles a day for 21 days. How many miles did he walk in all?
7. Round 743,214 to the nearest ten thousand.	8. $335 \times 5 =$
9. The area of a room in a dollhouse is 1,248 square inches. The width of the room is 8 inches. How long is the room?	10. Lisa played her new CD for 3 hours every day for the first 5 days she had it. How many total hours did she play the CD? How many minutes was this?

4.OA.1, 4.OA.2, 4.OA.3, 4.OA.5, 4.NBT.3, 4.NBT.4, 4.NBT.5, 4.NBT.6, 4.MD.3   CD-104593 • © Carson-Dellosa

Name_____

Day 1

Grantsville's governor received 3 times as many votes as Cary's governor. Cary's governor received 790 votes. How many people voted altogether?

Dylan plants grass in a rectangular space behind the clubhouse. The area of the space is 70 square feet. If the length of the space is 14 feet, what is the width of the space?

Day 2

Ruby baked 5 apple pies for a bake sale. If each pie contained 12 apples, how many total apples did Ruby use?

Start at 4. Create a pattern that multiplies each number by 4 and then adds 3. Stop when you have 5 numbers.

Write the number in standard form.

900,00 + 80,000 + 500 + 7

$774 \times 6 =$

Round 54,678 to the nearest ten.

$286 \div 8 =$

Day 3

Write the equation.

During lunch, some students eat 32 bags of pretzel rods. If each bag holds 9 pretzel rods, how many total pretzel rods do the students eat?

Write <, >, or = to make the statement true.

76,876 ◯ 76,768

Day 4

$147 \times 2 =$

$67,987 - 32,998 =$

Write the number in expanded form.

76,789

$868 \div 4 =$

$500 \div 50 =$

A rectangular closet has a perimeter of 10 feet. If the width of the closet is 3 feet, what is the length of the closet?

---

1. The area of a bathroom floor is 24 square feet. If the width of the bathroom is 6 feet, what is the length of the bathroom?

2. $639 \times 9 =$

3. Six times as many people voted in the 2012 election as in the 2008 election. If 162 people voted in 2008, how many people voted in both elections?

4. A rectangular bedroom has a perimeter of 42 feet. If the length of the bedroom is 11 feet, what is the width of the bedroom?

5. Start at 2. Create a pattern that adds 2 to each number and then multiplies by 3. Stop when you have 5 numbers.

6. $67,545 - 33,878 =$

7. $370 \div 4 =$

8. Tyler made 6 batches of biscuits. He made 24 biscuits in each batch. How many total biscuits did Tyler make?

9. Write the equation.

   Lisa made 18 blueberry muffins. If each muffin contained 6 blueberries, how many total blueberries did Lisa use?

10. Round 55,678 to the nearest hundred.

4.OA.1, 4.OA.2, 4.OA.3, 4.OA.5, 4.NBT.3, 4.NBT.4, 4.NBT.5, 4.NBT.6, 4.MD.3

Name_____

Day 1

5,001 × 6 =	Write the equation. Jessi has saved $51. If Lee has saved 5 times as much money as Jessi, how much money has Lee saved?
413,206 − 78,598 =	The area of a rectangle is 116 square meters. If the length of the rectangle is 4 meters, what is the width of the rectangle?

Day 2

8,867 × 5 =	Write the number word as a number. five thousand eight hundred ninety-two
List the factors of 68. Is this number prime or composite?	The perimeter of the top of a desk is 54 inches. If the length of the desk is 15 inches, what is the width of the desk?

Day 3

486 ÷ 6 =	Round 248,739 to the nearest hundred.
Start at 1,000. Create a pattern that subtracts 8 from each number. Stop when you have 5 numbers.	Lauren is moving on Saturday. She has packed 8 boxes in each room in her house. She has 5 rooms in her house. How many boxes has Lauren packed in all?

Day 4

774 ÷ 6 =	43,204 + 23,524 =
375,211 − 188,456 =	Peter attends 6 dance lessons each week, all year long. A year has 52 weeks. Peter missed 5 dance lessons while sick. How many dance lessons did Peter attend during the year?

1. $4,114 \times 8 =$

2. The perimeter of the cover of a math textbook is 34 inches. If the width of the cover is 7 inches, what is the length of the cover?

3. Julio is training for a marathon. He runs 34 miles the first week and 29 miles the next week. During the third week, he wants to run as many miles as he ran the first 2 weeks combined. He plans to run an equal number of miles during each of the 7 days of the week. How many miles will Julio run each day?

4. Write the number word as a number.

   three hundred forty-two thousand six hundred eight

5. Write the equation.

   Madeline spends 4 hours at the gym each week. How much time does she spend at the gym in an 8-week period?

6. $192 \div 12 =$

7. The area of a rectangle is 336 square inches. If the width of the rectangle is 6 inches. What is the length of the rectangle?

8. $68,242 + 35,254 =$

9. List the factors of 67.

   Is this number prime or composite?

10. A sold-out concert is playing at Sunset Gardens on Friday, Saturday, and Sunday nights. A total of 779 tickets were sold for each night of the performance. How many tickets were sold for the 3 nights in all?

Day 1

$91 \times 17 =$

$754,326 - 561,268 =$

The area of a rectangular ice-skating rink is 900 square yards. If the length of the rink is 100 yards, what is the width of the rink?

Write the equation.

Lucy rides her bike 20 kilometers every week. How many kilometers does Lucy ride her bike in 7 weeks?

Day 2

$576 \div 5 =$

$173,249 + 56,245 =$

Round 462,145 to the nearest ten.

A total of 419 students will attend Field Day. Mr. Wolf needs 4 ribbons for each student and 48 ribbons for the parents who will be helping. How many ribbons does Mr. Wolf need in all?

Day 3

Start at 92. Create a pattern that adds 13 to each number. Stop when you have 5 numbers.

$80 \div 8 =$

$77 \times 80 =$

The movie theater had 135 people in it. If the people split into 9 even groups to watch different movies, how many people will watch each movie?

Day 4

Write the number in word form.

50,328

The perimeter of a sheet of paper is 38 centimeters. If the width of the paper is 8 centimeters, what is the length of the paper?

$140 \div 4 =$

$38 \times 24 =$

1. $87 \times 80 =$

2. $105 \div 8 =$

3. The perimeter of a deck is 30 feet. If the length of the deck is 10 feet, what is the width of the deck?

4. Nadia, Jimmy, and Terrance collected 769 stickers during the school year. They want to divide the stickers equally. They plan to give any leftover stickers to Vanessa. How many stickers will each person get?

5. In April, 287 people visited an amusement park. In May, 379 people visited the same amusement park. In June, twice as many people visited the amusement park as visited in April and May combined. How many people visited the amusement park in June?

6. $324,159 - 278,634 =$

7. The area of Brooke's vegetable garden is 40 square feet. If the width of the garden is 8 feet, what is the length of the garden?

8. $300 \div 30 =$

9. Write the number in word form.

   503,208

10. Write the equation.

   Kennedy earns $8 each time she babysits her little sister Leslie. If Kennedy babysits Leslie 9 times, how much money will she earn?

4.OA.1, 4.OA.2, 4.OA.3, 4.NBT.1, 4.NBT.4, 4.NBT.5, 4.NBT.6, 4.MD.3 CD-104593 • © Carson-Dellosa

Day 1

The movie theater had 352 people in it. If the people split into 8 even groups to watch different movies, how many people will watch each movie?

543,286 + 215,740 =

Write the number in expanded form.

seven hundred twenty-one thousand nine hundred four

The perimeter of a rectangle is 222 millimeters. If the length of the rectangle is 60 millimeters, what is the width of the rectangle?

Day 2

Write the equation.

During the year, Myong travels 5,678 miles by airplane. He travels twice as many miles by train. How many miles does Myong travel by train?

Jacob and Dustin collected 245 cans for the school can drive. They gave 55 cans to Dustin's little sister for her class to get credit. How many cans does this leave for the boys' class?

700,000 ÷ 70,000 =

1,002 ÷ 2 =

Day 3

Rudy has 10 white seashells, 23 pink seashells, and 21 brown seashells. If he divides his seashells equally between 3 friends, how many seashells will each friend get?

Round 213,548 to the nearest hundred thousand.

Determine the 30th shape in the pattern.

89 × 55 =

Day 4

The area of a rectangle is 1,035 square centimeters. If the length of the rectangle is 3 centimeters, what is the width of the rectangle?

Write <, >, or = to make the statement true.

94,306 ◯ 94,360

List the factors of 75.

Is this number prime or composite?

2,002 × 4 =

1. 4,012 ÷ 2 =

2. The area of a rectangle is 6,384 square yards. If the width of the rectangle is 7 yards, what is the length of the rectangle?

3. The movie theater donated 648 tickets to 9 schools. If the movie theater donated the same number of tickets to each school, how many tickets did each school receive?

4. 35 × 96 =

5. 49,320 + 36,249 =

6. Round 743,214 to the nearest ten thousand.

7. A blue whale traveled 495 feet the first time it was sighted. The second time it was sighted, the blue whale had traveled 6 times as far as the first time. How far did the blue whale travel altogether?

8. 6,567 × 3 =

9. The perimeter of a rectangle is 154 feet. The length of the rectangle is 55 feet. What is the width of the rectangle?

10. Write the equation.

Mrs. Chung has 33 students in her fourth-grade class. Her students are making collages on Friday, so she brings in 5 magazines for each student. How many magazines does Mrs. Chung bring to class?

Day 1

96 × 22 =

Write the number word as a number.

eight hundred twenty thousand five hundred fifteen

Write the equation.

Jack saw 4 times as many footballs as soccer balls in the store. Jack saw 234 soccer balls. How many footballs did Jack see?

The area of a rectangle is 228 square feet. If the length of the rectangle is 12 feet, what is the width of the rectangle?

Day 2

2,123 × 4 =

Round 247,596 to the nearest thousand.

Write <, >, or = to make the statement true.

62,381 ◯ 62,831

The perimeter of a rectangle is 62 feet. If the width of the rectangle is 19 feet, what is the length of the rectangle?

Day 3

728 ÷ 8 =

624,193 + 353,126 =

50 ÷ 5 =

Liza works 7 hours a day, 7 days a week. How many hours does Liza work in 6 weeks?

Day 4

224 ÷ 5 =

954,328 − 864,597 =

Start at 12. Create a pattern that multiplies each number by 4. Stop when you have 5 numbers.

The reptile house at the zoo has 245 reptiles. Each habitat holds 5 reptiles. How many habitats are there?

1. Riley's class takes a field trip to a museum. Riley sees 116 exhibits total. Each room has 4 exhibits in it. How many rooms does Riley go through?

2. $768 \div 4 =$

3. Write the number word as a number.

   forty-three thousand sixteen

4. Noah rides bikes 15 miles a day, 5 days a week. How many miles does Noah bike in 8 weeks?

5. The area of Ava's rectangular backyard is 325 square yards. If the length of the yard is 13 yards, what is the width of the yard?

6. Round 329,167 to the nearest hundred.

7. $743,245 - 368,195 =$

8. Write the equation.

   In winter, a sporting goods store sells 5 times as many snowboards as it sells during summer. The store sells 132 snowboards in summer. How many snowboards does the store sell in winter?

9. $87 \times 47 =$

10. The perimeter of Lola's rectangular backyard is 76 feet. If the width of the yard is 25 feet, what is the length of the yard?

4.OA.1, 4.OA.2, 4.OA.3, 4.NBT.2, 4.NBT.3, 4.NBT.4, 4.NBT.5, 4.NBT.6, 4.MD.3   CD-104593 • © Carson-Dellosa

Name_____

Day 1

$6{,}312 \div 8 =$	List the factors of 61. Is this number prime or composite?
Round 241,458 to the nearest ten.	The perimeter of a kitchen is 528 inches. If the width of the kitchen is 120 inches, what is the length of the kitchen?

Day 2

$38 \times 27 =$	Start at 7. Create a pattern that multiplies by 7. Stop when you have 5 numbers.
$753{,}091 + 173{,}256 =$	Sam has 26 yellow fish, 19 blue fish, and 43 orange fish. He has 8 fish tanks. If he divides the fish equally between the tanks, how many fish are in each tank?

Day 3

$600{,}000 \div 60{,}000 =$	$5{,}206 \times 3 =$
$489 \div 8 =$	Iesha needed more room in her closet. She decided to take half of her outfits to the attic closet. She had a total of 42 outfits. How many outfits did she move to the attic?

Day 4

The area of the top of a rectangular table is 323 square feet. If the length of the table is 19 feet, what is the width of the table?	Write the number in word form. 841,504
$75 \times 36 =$	Write the equation. Grace saw 16 bird habitats at the zoo's aviary. The sign said each habitat had 12 birds. How many birds were in the aviary in all?

1. Travis had a birthday party and invited 9 friends. He had 360 baseball cards to give away as party favors. How many baseball cards did each friend receive if Travis gave away all of his cards?

2. List the factors of 70.

   Is this number prime or composite?

3. The area of a bookshelf is 216 square inches. If the length of the bookshelf is 36 inches, what is the width of the bookshelf?

4. $57 \times 16 =$

5. Start at 158. Create a pattern that adds 8. Stop when you have 5 numbers.

6. Chloe has $15 to spend on pencils. Each box of pencils costs $2. How many boxes of pencils can Chloe buy? How much money does Chloe have left after she buys the pencils?

7. $2,537 \div 7 =$

8. The perimeter of a living room is 68 feet. If the length of the living room is 18 feet, what is the width of the living room?

9. Write the equation.

   Nell sold 125 packages of cookies at the bake sale. Each package was tied with 2 ribbons. How many ribbons were used in all?

10. $485,122 + 512,137 =$

 CD-104593 • © Carson-Dellosa

Name_____

Day 1 Lisa earned $31 each week for delivering newspapers. She delivered newspapers for 2 weeks. How much money did Lisa earn?	$22 \times 44 =$	**Day 2** Britney wants to buy 2 shirts that are on sale. Each shirt is on sale for $14, including tax. If Britney has $30, how much change will she get after buying the shirts?	$30 \times 30 =$
$880,372 - 751,684 =$	The area of a dog kennel is 20 square feet. If the length of the kennel is 4 feet, what is the width of the kennel?	$800 \div 80 =$	Write <, >, or = to make the statement true. 136,284 ◯ 134,284
Day 3 Write the equation. The Iowa candidate got 6 times as many votes as the Ohio candidate. The Ohio candidate got 850 votes. How many votes did the Iowa candidate get?	$2,995 \times 7 =$	**Day 4** The perimeter of a rectangular window is 634 inches. If the length of the window is 205 inches, what is the width of the window?	$8,329 \div 9 =$
Round 463,462 to the nearest ten thousand.	$1,350 \div 6 =$	Write the number in standard form. $700,000 + 20,000 + 2,000 + 100 + 70$	$85,911 + 28,347 =$

---

1. Carrie buys 13 picture frames for $12 each, including tax. If Carrie has $160, how much change will she get back after she buys the picture frames?

2. $43 \times 23 =$

---

3. $3,400 \div 5 =$

4. Write the equation.

Ursula polled her classmates to see what their favorite kinds of juice were. Eight times as many students voted for grape as orange. Forty-three students voted for orange. How many students voted for grape?

---

5. Rosa makes a small flower garden outside the clubhouse. The area of the garden is 851 square meters. If the length of the garden is 23 meters, what is the width of the garden?

6. $90 \div 9 =$

---

7. Write <, >, or = to make the statement true.

603,897 $\bigcirc$ 630,897

8. On each table, Tiffany displayed 13 crafts. If she had 8 tables, how many crafts did Tiffany display?

---

9. The perimeter of a picture frame is 24 inches. If the width of the picture frame is 5 inches, what is the length of the picture frame?

10. $2,310 \div 5 =$

4.OA.1, 4.OA.2, 4.OA.3, 4.NBT.1, 4.NBT.2, 4.NBT.5, 4.NBT.6, 4.MD.3 CD-104593 • © Carson-Dellosa

Name_____

Day 1

Write <, >, or = to make the statement true.

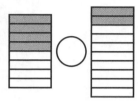

Write the equation.

Emory picked 9 daisies. Ginny picked 7 times more daisies than Emory. How many daisies did Ginny pick?

Day 2

$\frac{3}{5} + \frac{1}{5} =$

Abbie bought 82 cases of water for her restaurant. Each case had 24 bottles of water. How many bottles of water did Abbie buy in all?

Start at 4. Create a pattern that multiplies each number by 5. Stop when you have 5 numbers.

If it takes Tracy $\frac{1}{4}$ of an hour to do her homework, and it takes Trent $\frac{3}{4}$ of an hour to do his homework, how much total time does it take Tracy and Trent to do their homework?

$9,000 \div 900 =$

If $\frac{3}{10} = \frac{30}{100}$,

then $\frac{4}{10} = \frac{\boxed{}}{100}$.

Day 3

Decompose $\frac{3}{5}$ in two ways.

A. $\frac{1}{5} + \frac{\boxed{}}{5} + \frac{\boxed{}}{5} = \frac{3}{5}$

B. $\frac{2}{5} + \frac{\boxed{}}{5} = \frac{3}{5}$

Henry has 342 marbles in bags. If 9 marbles are in each bag, how many bags does Henry have? How many bags will he have if he gives 15 bags to his brother?

Day 4

$3\frac{1}{3} + 2\frac{1}{3} =$

List the factors of 38.

Is this number prime or composite?

Write <, >, or = to make the statement true.

136,284 $\bigcirc$ 136,248

If the fraction $\frac{6}{10}$ equals 0.6, then $\frac{5}{10}$ equals _____ .

Write the number in word form.

83,602

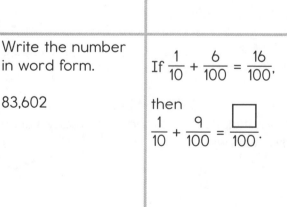

49

1. Write <, >, or = to make the statement true.

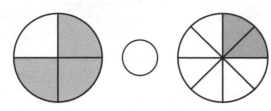

2. $\frac{1}{3} + \frac{1}{3} =$

3. Decompose $\frac{5}{6}$ in two ways.

A. $\frac{1}{6} + \frac{\square}{6} + \frac{\square}{6} + \frac{\square}{6} + \frac{\square}{6} = \frac{5}{6}$

B. $\frac{3}{6} + \frac{\square}{6} + \frac{\square}{6} = \frac{5}{6}$

4. $4\frac{2}{5} + \frac{1}{5} =$

5. If it takes Tracy $\frac{2}{4}$ of an hour to clean a bathroom, and it takes Trent $\frac{1}{4}$ of an hour to clean a bathroom, how much total time does it take Tracy and Trent to clean the bathrooms?

6. If $\frac{2}{10} = \frac{20}{100}$, then $\frac{5}{10} = \frac{\square}{100}$.

7. If the fraction $\frac{4}{10}$ equals 0.4, then $\frac{8}{10}$ equals _____ .

8. If $\frac{2}{10} + \frac{2}{100} = \frac{22}{100}$, then $\frac{4}{10} + \frac{5}{100} = \frac{\square}{100}$.

9. Write the equation.

Delinda won 8 tickets. Ivan won 8 times as many tickets as Delinda. How many tickets did Ivan win?

10. A moving company is able to move 92 boxes every hour. How many boxes are they able to move during an 8-hour workday?

Day 1

Round 543,873 to the nearest ten thousand.

$1,152 \div 6 =$

Day 2

$13,954 + 5,268 =$

The area of a rectangle is 1,176 square meters. The width of the rectangle is 21 meters. What is the length of the rectangle?

The brown horse runs $\frac{3}{12}$ of a mile. The black horse runs $\frac{4}{12}$ of a mile. How many miles total do the black and brown horses run?

Write <, >, or = to make the statement true.

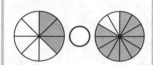

If $\frac{3}{10} = \frac{30}{100}$, then $\frac{8}{10} = \frac{\square}{100}$.

$\frac{1}{6} + \frac{3}{6} =$

Day 3

$681 \times 3 =$

$690 \div 4 =$

Day 4

$56 \times 22 =$

The perimeter of a rectangle is 60 meters. If the length of the rectangle is 14 meters, what is the width of the rectangle?

If $\frac{4}{10} + \frac{5}{100} = \frac{45}{100}$, then $\frac{7}{10} + \frac{7}{100} = \frac{\square}{100}$.

Decompose $\frac{3}{5}$ in two ways.

A. $\frac{1}{3} + \frac{\square}{3} + \frac{\square}{3} = \frac{3}{3}$

B. $\frac{1}{3} + \frac{\square}{3} = \frac{3}{3}$

If the fraction $\frac{26}{100}$ equals 0.26, then $\frac{33}{100}$ equals _____.

$3\frac{3}{8} + 2\frac{5}{8} =$

1. Round 687,155 to the nearest ten.

2. 2,594 + 15,507 =

3. If $\frac{16}{100}$ equals 0.16,

then $\frac{87}{100}$ equals _____ .

4. If $\frac{1}{10} + \frac{1}{100} = \frac{11}{100}$, then $\frac{4}{10} + \frac{8}{100} = \frac{\square}{100}$.

5. If $\frac{5}{10} = \frac{50}{100}$, then $\frac{9}{10} = \frac{\square}{100}$.

6. Kayla runs $\frac{5}{10}$ of a mile, and Jason runs $\frac{4}{10}$ of a mile. How many miles total do Kayla and Jason run?

7. $2\frac{4}{5} + 3\frac{2}{5} =$

8. Decompose $\frac{4}{12}$ in two ways.

A. $\frac{1}{12} + \frac{\square}{12} + \frac{\square}{12} + \frac{\square}{12} = \frac{4}{12}$

B. $\frac{2}{12} + \frac{\square}{12} = \frac{4}{12}$

9. $\frac{1}{7} + \frac{2}{7} =$

10. Write <, >, or = to make the statement true.

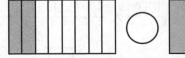 

4.NBT.3, 4.NBT.4, 4.NF.2, 4.NF.3, 4.NF.5, 4.NF.6

Name_____

Day 1

$13\frac{5}{8} + \frac{7}{8} =$

List the factors of 34.

Is this number prime or composite?

Day 2

Decompose $\frac{3}{8}$ in two ways.

A. $\frac{1}{8} + \frac{\square}{8} + \frac{\square}{8} = \frac{3}{8}$

B. $\frac{2}{8} + \frac{\square}{8} = \frac{3}{8}$

Forrest orders 5 boxes of toothbrushes. If he has 135 toothbrushes altogether, how many are in each box?

Determine the 13th shape in the pattern.

If $\frac{6}{10} + \frac{5}{100} = \frac{65}{100}$,

then $\frac{5}{10} + \frac{2}{100} = \frac{\square}{100}$.

$10 \div 1 =$

If the fraction $\frac{55}{100}$ equals 0.55, then $\frac{64}{100}$ equals _____.

Day 3

$\frac{1}{4} + \frac{1}{4} =$

Ellen has 150 CDs. She wants to store an equal number of CDs in 2 containers. How many CDs should Ellen put in each container?

Day 4

Write <, >, or = to make the statement true.

$\frac{1}{5} \bigcirc \frac{2}{10}$

Write the equation.

Gregory is 2 years old. His aunt is 12 times his age. How old is Gregory's aunt?

Write the number word as a number.

eighty-nine thousand nine hundred eighty

If $\frac{4}{10} = \frac{40}{100}$,

then $\frac{7}{10} = \frac{\square}{100}$.

Round 15,454 to the nearest thousand.

The recipe for Ryan's birthday cake calls for $\frac{3}{4}$ of a cup of flour and $\frac{2}{4}$ of a cup of sugar. How many total cups of flour and sugar does the recipe call for?

---

1. Miguel orders 595 candy bars. They come in 7 boxes. How many candy bars are in each box? How many candy bars will he have left if he gives 3 boxes to his friend?

2. List the factors of 16.

   Is this number prime or composite?

3. If $\frac{3}{10} + \frac{6}{100} = \frac{36}{100}$, then $\frac{8}{10} + \frac{3}{100} = \frac{\boxed{}}{100}$.

4. If the fraction $\frac{71}{100}$ equals 0.71, then $\frac{49}{100}$ equals _____.

5. Write <, >, or = to make the statement true.

   $\frac{3}{12} \bigcirc \frac{1}{3}$

6. $\frac{1}{12} + \frac{4}{12} =$

7. Decompose $\frac{7}{8}$ in two ways.

   A. $\frac{3}{8} + \frac{\boxed{}}{8} = \frac{7}{8}$

   B. $\frac{2}{8} + \frac{\boxed{}}{8} = \frac{7}{8}$

8. $1\frac{3}{4} + 2\frac{3}{4} =$

9. Ryan adds $\frac{5}{8}$ of a cup of applesauce to his cake recipe. He then measures and adds $\frac{1}{8}$ of a cup more of applesauce. How much applesauce has Ryan added to his cake altogether?

10. If $\frac{5}{10} = \frac{50}{100}$, then $\frac{6}{10} = \frac{\boxed{}}{100}$.

4.OA.3, 4.OA.4, 4.NF.2, 4.NF.3, 4.NF.5, 4.NF.6   CD-104593 • © Carson-Dellosa

Name_____

Day 1

$3\frac{5}{6} + 2\frac{3}{6} =$

$16{,}081 + 36{,}584 =$

$\frac{1}{6} + \frac{4}{6} =$

$\frac{3}{10} + \frac{3}{100} = \dfrac{\square}{100}$

Day 2

$\frac{3}{6} + \frac{2}{6} =$

$34 \times 12 =$

$\frac{4}{12} - \frac{2}{12} =$

Write the decimal.

$\frac{7}{10} = $ _____

Day 3

Write <, >, or = to make the statement true.

$\frac{5}{10} \bigcirc \frac{3}{6}$

$342 \div 6 =$

Write the decimal.

$\frac{32}{100} = $ _____

The Rossi family ate $\frac{1}{3}$ of a cheese pizza and $\frac{2}{3}$ of a vegetarian pizza. How much total pizza did the Rossi family eat?

Day 4

Decompose $\frac{5}{10}$ in two ways.

A. $\frac{2}{10} + \dfrac{\square}{10} = \frac{5}{10}$

B. $\frac{1}{10} + \dfrac{\square}{10} = \frac{5}{10}$

The perimeter of a rectangular sandbox is 34 feet. If the length of the sandbox is 8 feet, what is the width of the sandbox?

$4{,}876 \times 6 =$

$\dfrac{\square}{10} = \frac{40}{100}$

Name_____

1. $21 \times 31 =$

2. Write <, >, or = to make the statement true.

$$\frac{3}{6} \bigcirc \frac{4}{8}$$

3. $1,505 \div 5 =$

4. $\dfrac{3}{8} + \dfrac{3}{8} =$

5. Write the decimal.

$$\frac{14}{100} = \underline{\hspace{2cm}}$$

6. Decompose $\dfrac{3}{4}$ in two ways.

A. $\dfrac{1}{4} + \dfrac{\boxed{}}{4} = \dfrac{3}{4}$

B. $\dfrac{1}{4} + \dfrac{\boxed{}}{4} + \dfrac{\boxed{}}{4} = \dfrac{3}{4}$

7. $\dfrac{1}{10} + \dfrac{6}{100} = \dfrac{\boxed{}}{100}$

8. $2\dfrac{7}{10} + 1\dfrac{4}{10} =$

9. $\dfrac{\boxed{}}{10} = \dfrac{70}{100}$

10. The Freeman family ate $\dfrac{2}{6}$ of a sausage pizza and $\dfrac{3}{6}$ of a cheese pizza. How much total pizza did the Freeman family eat?

4.NBT.5, 4.NBT.6, 4.NF.2, 4.NF.3, 4.NF.5, 4.NF.6

Name_____

Day 1

The mayor of Glenville Heights gave 3 flags to every person in his community. Glenville Heights has 1,298 people. How many flags did the mayor give away in all?

$$\frac{\square}{10} = \frac{20}{100}$$

$$\frac{3}{12} + \frac{5}{12} =$$

$875 \div 7 =$

Day 2

$2,005 \times 5 =$

Ross ate $\frac{3}{10}$ of a pumpkin pie. Brady ate $\frac{6}{10}$ of the same pie. How much of the pie did Ross and Brady eat altogether?

Write <, >, or = to make the statement true.

$$\frac{3}{5} \bigcirc \frac{1}{2}$$

$20,000 \div 2,000 =$

Day 3

$56,877 - 45,996 =$

$$\frac{9}{10} + \frac{9}{100} =$$

$$5\frac{4}{8} + \frac{2}{8} =$$

Write <, >, or = to make the statement true.

$$98,509 \bigcirc 98,905$$

Day 4

Jake's dog weighs 24 pounds. Liv's dog weighs 42 pounds. Jimmy's dog weighs twice as much as Jake's and Liv's dogs combined. How much does Jimmy's dog weigh?

Write the decimal.

$$\frac{54}{100} = \underline{\hspace{2cm}}$$

Decompose $\frac{7}{10}$ in two ways.

A. $\dfrac{\square}{10} + \dfrac{\square}{10} = \dfrac{7}{10}$

B. $\dfrac{\square}{10} + \dfrac{\square}{10} = \dfrac{7}{10}$

Round 320,152 to the nearest ten.

Name_____

1.
Ansley ate $\frac{3}{12}$ of a bag of popcorn. Erica ate $\frac{4}{12}$ of the same bag of popcorn. What fraction of the bag of popcorn did Ansley and Erica eat in all?

2.
$$\frac{\square}{10} = \frac{80}{100}$$

3.
$$3\frac{7}{12} + 4\frac{9}{12} =$$

4.
$$\frac{7}{10} + \frac{1}{100} = \frac{\square}{100}$$

5.
Decompose $\frac{4}{8}$ in two ways.

A. $\dfrac{\square}{8} + \dfrac{\square}{8} = \dfrac{4}{8}$

B. $\dfrac{\square}{8} + \dfrac{\square}{8} = \dfrac{4}{8}$

6. Write the decimal.
$$\frac{26}{100} = \underline{\hspace{2cm}}$$

7.
$$\frac{6}{8} + \frac{1}{8} =$$

8. Perry has 135 books. If they are in 3 boxes, how many books are in each box? How many books will he have left if he donates 1 box of books to the library?

9. Write <, >, or = to make the statement true.

$$\frac{2}{3} \bigcirc \frac{5}{8}$$

10. $40,000 \div 4,000 =$

4.OA.3, 4.NBT.1, 4.NF.2, 4.NF.3, 4.NF.5, 4.NF.6   CD-104593 • © Carson-Dellosa

Day 1

If $\frac{4}{5} = 4 \times (\frac{1}{5})$,

then

$\frac{4}{6} = \boxed{} \times (\frac{\boxed{}}{\boxed{}})$.

John eats $\frac{4}{12}$ of a sandwich. Emma eats $\frac{3}{12}$ of the same sandwich. How much more sandwich did John eat than Emma?

Day 2

$3 \times \frac{2}{3} =$

$\frac{\boxed{}}{10} = \frac{50}{100}$

List the factors of 90.

Is this number prime or composite?

Write <, >, or = to make the statement true.

$\frac{1}{3} \bigcirc \frac{2}{5}$

Owen's bedroom has a perimeter of 46 feet. If the length of the bedroom is 11 feet, what is the width of the bedroom?

$\frac{3}{8} - \frac{1}{8} =$

Day 3

Each person at a party will eat $\frac{2}{3}$ of a pound of turkey, and 8 people will be at the party. How many pounds of turkey will be needed?

$\frac{2}{10} + \frac{5}{100} = \frac{\boxed{}}{100}$

Day 4

Write <, >, or = to make the statement true.

$0.2 \bigcirc 0.4$

Write the decimal.

$\frac{6}{100} =$ _____

$25,694 + 15,507 =$

Decompose $\frac{9}{12}$ in two ways.

A. $\frac{\boxed{}}{12} + \frac{\boxed{}}{12} = \frac{9}{12}$

B. $\frac{\boxed{}}{12} + \frac{\boxed{}}{12} = \frac{9}{12}$

Write the equation.

Vanessa has 10 stickers. Tara has 6 times as many stickers as Vanessa. How many stickers does Tara have?

$5\frac{1}{3} - 2\frac{2}{3} =$

1.

If $\frac{4}{5} = 4 \times (\frac{1}{5})$, then $\frac{6}{10} = \boxed{} \times (\frac{\boxed{}}{\boxed{}})$.

2.

$2 \times \frac{4}{5} =$

3.

Each student needs $\frac{2}{5}$ of a cup of play dough to build a house. How many cups of play dough are needed for 9 students?

4. Write <, >, or = to make the statement true.

0.15 $\bigcirc$ 0.10

5. Write <, >, or = to make the statement true.

$\frac{3}{5}$ $\bigcirc$ $\frac{2}{3}$

6.

$\frac{3}{8} - \frac{1}{8} =$

7.

Decompose $\frac{5}{5}$ in two ways.

A. $\frac{\boxed{}}{5} + \frac{\boxed{}}{5} = \frac{5}{5}$

B. $\frac{\boxed{}}{5} + \frac{\boxed{}}{5} = \frac{5}{5}$

8.

$4\frac{1}{6} - 3\frac{5}{6} =$

9.

Holly took $\frac{2}{8}$ of a pan of brownies. Ivan took $\frac{5}{8}$ of a pan of brownies. How much more of the pan of brownies did Ivan take than Holly?

10.

$\frac{\boxed{}}{10} = \frac{90}{100}$

4.NF.2, 4.NF.3, 4.NF.4, 4.NF.5, 4.NF.7

Name_____

Day 1

Write the decimal.

$\frac{68}{100} = $ _____

$6\frac{3}{5} - 3\frac{1}{5} =$

$934 \times 6 =$

Write <, >, or = to make the statement true.

$0.46 \bigcirc 0.32$

Day 2

If $\frac{4}{5} = 4 \times (\frac{1}{5})$,

then

$\frac{2}{8} = \square \times (\frac{\square}{\square})$.

Connor ate $\frac{1}{4}$ of an apple. Orlando ate $\frac{1}{4}$ of the same apple. How much of the apple did Connor and Orlando eat in all?

$3{,}744 \div 8 =$

Write <, >, or = to make the statement true.

$\frac{7}{10} \bigcirc \frac{2}{3}$

Day 3

$6 \times \frac{2}{5} =$

$\frac{2}{10} = \frac{\square}{100}$

April has 394 paper clips that she has to divide equally between 9 of her coworkers. How many paper clips will each coworker get from April? How many paper clips will be left?

$\frac{2}{6} - \frac{1}{6} =$

Day 4

Mrs. Benson must give each child $\frac{2}{12}$ of a pizza. She is feeding 4 children, How much pizza does Mrs. Benson have to make?

$\frac{6}{10} + \frac{8}{100} = \frac{\square}{100}$

Write the number in expanded form.

eight hundred forty thousand three

Decompose $\frac{4}{8}$ in two ways.

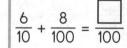

A. $\frac{\square}{8} + \frac{\square}{8} = \frac{4}{8}$

B. $\frac{\square}{8} + \frac{\square}{8} = \frac{4}{8}$

Name_____

1.

$\frac{3}{10} = \frac{\square}{100}$

2. Write <, >, or = to make the statement true.

0.95 $\bigcirc$ 0.99

3.

$4\frac{7}{10} - 3\frac{3}{10} =$

4.

Mr. Lang must give each child $\frac{4}{6}$ of a cup of juice. How much juice does Mr. Lang have to buy for 4 children?

5.

Decompose $\frac{6}{8}$ in two ways.

A. $\frac{\square}{8} + \frac{\square}{8} = \frac{6}{8}$

B. $\frac{\square}{8} + \frac{\square}{8} = \frac{6}{8}$

6.

$3 \times \frac{3}{10} =$

7.

$\frac{4}{6} - \frac{2}{6} =$

8.

If $\frac{4}{5} = 4 \times (\frac{1}{5})$, then $\frac{2}{4} = \square \times (\frac{\square}{\square})$.

9. Write <, >, or = to make the statement true.

$\frac{3}{10} \bigcirc \frac{2}{5}$

10. Write the decimal.

$\frac{29}{100} =$ _____

4.NF.2, 4.NF.3, 4.NF.4, 4.NF.5, 4.NF.6, 4.NF.7

Name_____

Day 1

If $\frac{4}{5} = 4 \times (\frac{1}{5})$,

then

$\frac{7}{3} = \square \times (\frac{\square}{\square})$.

Uri shared $\frac{6}{8}$ of his orange with his friend and ate the rest. How much of the orange did Uri eat?

Day 2

$9 \times \frac{3}{4} =$

Write the decimal.

$\frac{4}{10} =$ _____

Start at 4. Create a pattern that multiplies each number by 4. Stop when you have 5 numbers.

Write <, >, or = to make the statement true.

$\frac{1}{2} \bigcirc 2\frac{2}{5}$

Round 188,206 to the nearest thousand.

$\frac{7}{12} - \frac{5}{12} =$

Day 3

Shelby needs $\frac{4}{8}$ of a cup of oatmeal for each batch of cookies she is baking. If she wants to bake 7 batches of cookies, how much oatmeal will she need?

$\frac{1}{10} = \frac{\square}{100}$

Write <, >, or = to make the statement true.

$0.76 \bigcirc 0.67$

Day 4

$\frac{4}{10} + \frac{7}{100} = \frac{\square}{100}$

Kevin has 244 marshmallows. He drops 16. If 9 people share the remaining marshmallows, how many will each person get?

Decompose $\frac{3}{10}$ in two ways.

A. $\frac{\square}{10} + \frac{\square}{10} + \frac{\square}{10} = \frac{3}{10}$

B. $\frac{\square}{10} + \frac{\square}{10} = \frac{3}{10}$

Write the equation.

Colby has 8 gems. Evan has 3 times as many gems as Colby. How many gems does Evan have?

$8\frac{4}{5} - 5\frac{2}{5} =$

Name_____

1. Write <, >, or = to make the statement true.

$$\frac{2}{12} \bigcirc \frac{1}{2}$$

2. $\frac{5}{6} - \frac{1}{6} =$

3. Write <, >, or = to make the statement true.

$$0.89 \bigcirc 0.98$$

4. Decompose $\frac{4}{6}$ in two ways.

A. $\dfrac{\Box}{6} + \dfrac{\Box}{6} = \dfrac{4}{6}$

B. $\dfrac{\Box}{6} + \dfrac{\Box}{6} = \dfrac{4}{6}$

5. Wallace needs $\frac{7}{10}$ of a cup of pecans to make one pecan pie. If Wallace wants to make 4 pecan pies, how many cups of pecans will he need?

6. $3\frac{5}{8} - 2\frac{1}{8} =$

7. $8 \times \frac{1}{6} =$

8. Nicole washed $\frac{4}{10}$ of a bag of potatoes. She left the rest in a basket outside. What amount of potatoes did Nicole leave outside?

9. If $\frac{4}{5} = 4 \times (\frac{1}{5})$, then $\frac{10}{6} = \Box \times (\dfrac{\Box}{\Box})$.

10. Write the decimal.

$$\frac{36}{100} = \underline{\hspace{2cm}}$$

Name_____

Day 1

Sixty-five campers arrive. Nine go home early. If 8 people sleep in 1 tent, how many tents will the campers need?

Kim needs $\frac{2}{4}$ of a gallon of water for her balloon. Seth needs $\frac{3}{4}$ of a gallon of water for his balloon. How much more water does Seth need than Kim?

Day 2

$392,421 + 30,530 =$

If $\frac{4}{5} = 4 \times (\frac{1}{5})$,

then

$\frac{5}{12} = \square \times (\frac{\square}{\square})$.

Write <, >, or = to make the statement true.

$\frac{1}{4} \bigcirc \frac{3}{10}$

Write the decimal.

$\frac{28}{100} =$ _____

$\frac{9}{10} - \frac{4}{10} =$

$\frac{3}{10} = \frac{\square}{100}$

Day 3

Start at 200. Create a pattern that multiplies each number by 2. Stop when you have 5 numbers.

$6 \times \frac{1}{10} =$

Day 4

Round 139,664 to the nearest ten.

Vince needed $\frac{5}{8}$ of a package of marbles for each gift bag. If he had to make 5 gift bags, how many packages of marbles did Vince need?

Decompose $\frac{8}{10}$ in two ways.

A. $\frac{\square}{8} + \frac{\square}{8} = \frac{8}{10}$

B. $\frac{\square}{8} + \frac{\square}{8} = \frac{8}{10}$

$\frac{6}{10} + \frac{4}{100} = \frac{\square}{100}$

$12\frac{7}{12} - 10\frac{5}{12} =$

Write <, >, or = to make the statement true.

$0.3 \bigcirc 0.30$

Name_____

1. Write <, >, or = to make the statement true.

$$\frac{1}{2} \bigcirc \frac{5}{8}$$

2. $\frac{9}{8} - \frac{2}{8} =$

3. Decompose $\frac{7}{12}$ in two ways.

A. $\dfrac{\boxed{}}{12} + \dfrac{\boxed{}}{12} = \dfrac{7}{12}$

B. $\dfrac{\boxed{}}{12} + \dfrac{\boxed{}}{12} = \dfrac{7}{12}$

4. $6\frac{7}{10} - 2\frac{3}{10} =$

5. Wyatt ate $\frac{1}{12}$ of a banana. Shane ate $\frac{7}{12}$ of a banana. How much more banana did Shane eat than Wyatt?

6. If $\frac{4}{5} = 4 \times (\frac{1}{5})$, then $\frac{7}{8} = \boxed{} \times (\dfrac{\boxed{}}{\boxed{}})$.

7. $5 \times \frac{3}{10} =$

8. Nathan needs $\frac{1}{4}$ of a tablespoon of vanilla to make one milk shake. If Nathan wants to make 8 milk shakes, how much vanilla will he need?

9. Write <, >, or = to make the statement true.

$$0.6 \bigcirc 0.60$$

10. $\dfrac{3}{10} + \dfrac{9}{100} = \dfrac{\boxed{}}{100}$

4.NF.2, 4.NF.3, 4.NF.4, 4.NF.5, 4.NF.7

Day 1

Write <, >, or = to make the statement true.

$$\frac{2}{3} \bigcirc \frac{1}{2}$$

Write the decimal.

$$\frac{73}{100} = \underline{\hspace{2cm}}$$

Day 2

$$\frac{8}{10} - \frac{5}{10} =$$

$$\frac{\boxed{}}{10} = \frac{30}{100}$$

$1,176 \div 2 =$

Zane had $\frac{7}{8}$ of a bottle of water left. Ana had $\frac{4}{8}$ of a bottle of water left. How much more water did Zane have than Ana?

The candy jar has 251 pieces of candy. Roxanne adds 31 pieces of candy to it. If the candy is divided equally between 6 campers, how many pieces will each camper get?

If $\frac{4}{5} = 4 \times (\frac{1}{5})$,

then

$$\frac{6}{6} = \boxed{} \times (\frac{\boxed{}}{\boxed{}}).$$

Day 3

Decompose $\frac{11}{12}$ in two ways.

A. $\dfrac{\boxed{}}{12} + \dfrac{\boxed{}}{12} = \dfrac{11}{12}$

B. $\dfrac{\boxed{}}{12} + \dfrac{\boxed{}}{12} = \dfrac{11}{12}$

$$\frac{9}{10} + \frac{4}{100} = \frac{\boxed{}}{\boxed{}}$$

Day 4

$$4\frac{5}{6} - \frac{1}{6} =$$

Write <, >, or = to make the statement true.

$$0.45 \bigcirc 0.54$$

Round 324,145 to the nearest hundred thousand.

$$4 \times \frac{4}{8} =$$

Start at 820. Create a pattern that adds 30 to each number. Stop when you have 5 numbers.

Bonnie uses $\frac{2}{12}$ of a cup of sugar in each cupcake. If she is making 9 cupcakes, how much sugar will Bonnie need?

1. $\dfrac{8}{8} - \dfrac{2}{8} =$

2. $5\dfrac{2}{3} - 4 =$

3. If $\dfrac{4}{5} = 4 \times \left(\dfrac{1}{5}\right)$, then $\dfrac{9}{5} = \boxed{} \times \left(\dfrac{\boxed{}}{\boxed{}}\right)$.

4. Garrett is using $\dfrac{3}{4}$ of a tablespoon of barbecue sauce on each piece of chicken. If Garrett is making 8 pieces of chicken, how much barbecue sauce will he need?

5. Write <, >, or = to make the statement true.

$$0.38 \bigcirc 0.28$$

6. Write the decimal.

$$\dfrac{95}{100} = \underline{\qquad}$$

7. $7 \times \dfrac{1}{2} =$

8. Blake ate $\dfrac{4}{6}$ of his potpie. Claire ate $\dfrac{1}{6}$ of her potpie. How much more potpie did Blake eat than Claire?

9. Decompose $\dfrac{3}{12}$ in two ways.

A. $\dfrac{\boxed{}}{12} + \dfrac{\boxed{}}{12} + \dfrac{\boxed{}}{12} = \dfrac{3}{12}$

B. $\dfrac{\boxed{}}{12} + \dfrac{\boxed{}}{12} = \dfrac{3}{12}$

10. Write <, >, or = to make the statement true.

$$\dfrac{1}{2} \bigcirc \dfrac{4}{8}$$

4.NF.2, 4.NF.3, 4.NF.4, 4.NF.6, 4.NF.7

Name_____

Day 1

Complete the table.

m	cm
1	100
2	
3	
4	
5	
6	
7	

Draw an example of parallel lines.

3,766 ÷ 7 =

What is the value of the missing angle?

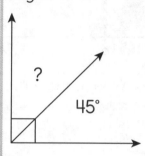

Day 2

James spends 45 minutes taking caring of Mr. Silva's dog. Then, he spends 25 minutes folding laundry. Next, he spends 20 minutes cleaning his room. How long does it take James to do all of his chores?

809,876 − 456,987 =

Write the number in standard form.

two hundred fifty-eight thousand six hundred eight

Color the right triangles.

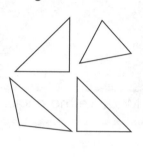

Day 3

Use the line plot below.

What is the difference in length between the longest and the shortest books?

Use the line plot below.

How many books measured 6 inches?

Lengths of Books on a Shelf in Inches

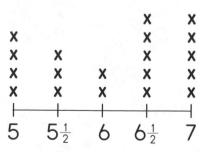

Day 4

9,876 × 8 =

Measure the angle.

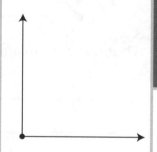

Circle the triangle that shows a line of symmetry.

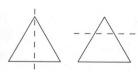

William, Jan, and Greg have a total of $26. Greg has the most money. Jan has twice as much money as William. Greg has $11. How much money does Jan have?

Name_____

---

1. 100 meters = _____ centimeters

2. Demetri wakes up at 9:15. It takes him 35 minutes to fold 4 loads of laundry, 35 minutes to bathe the dog, 45 minutes to bake brownies, and 1 hour to mow the lawn. After he finishes all of his chores, he sits down to rest. What time does Demetri rest?

---

3. Use the line plot below. What is the difference in length between the longest and the shortest book?

4. Use the line plot below. How many books measured 9 inches?

Lengths of Books on a Shelf in Inches

---

5. Measure the angle.

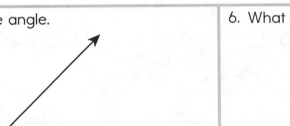

6. What is the value of the missing angle?

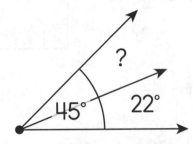

---

7. What is this an example of?

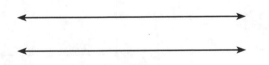

8. Draw a right triangle.

---

9. Draw the lines of symmetry on the airplane.

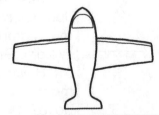

10. 786,987 − 43,786 =

Name_____

Day 1

Write the number word as a number.

three hundred fifty thousand seven

Color the shapes that have parallel lines.

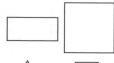

Day 2

Complete the table.

km	m
1	1,000
2	
3	
4	
5	
6	
7	

68,987 − 56,987 =

Measure the angle.

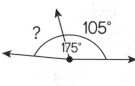

Madison packs 168 comic books into 8 different boxes. She packs an equal number of comic books in each box. How many comic books does Madison pack into each box?

7,648 ÷ 8 =

What kind of lines are shown?

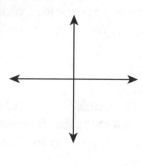

Day 3

85 × 66 =

Circle the figure that shows a line of symmetry.

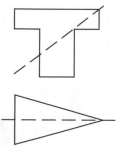

Day 4

Jeremy travels 16 kilometers total to and from school every day. How many kilometers does Jeremy travel to and from school in 20 days?

Round 532,453 to the nearest hundred thousand.

What is the value of the missing angle?

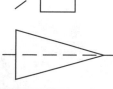
? 105°
175°

Start at 41. Create a pattern that multiplies each number by 3. Stop when you have 5 numbers.

$\frac{2}{4} + \frac{1}{4} =$

$6\frac{4}{8} + 1\frac{2}{8} =$

1. Scott's Pizzeria has 708 chairs. Four chairs are at each table. How many tables are in the restaurant?

2. 15 kilometers = _____ meters

3. Adam runs 135 kilometers over a 9-day period. It takes Adam about 10 minutes to run each kilometer. If Adam ran an equal number of kilometers each day, how many kilometers did Adam run each day? How much time did Adam spend running?

4. Round 456,755 to the nearest hundred thousand.

5. Start at 1,278. Create a pattern that subtracts 150 from each number. Stop when you have 5 numbers.

6. Measure the angle.

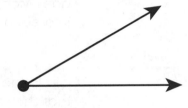

7. What is the value of the missing angle?

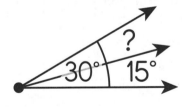
30° 15° ?

8. Draw perpendicular lines.

9. Draw two different figures that have parallel lines.

10. Draw the lines of symmetry on the shoe.

 CD-104593 • © Carson-Dellosa

Name_____

Day 1

Measure the angle.

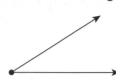

Decompose $\frac{5}{8}$ in two ways.

A. $\frac{\boxed{}}{8} + \frac{\boxed{}}{8} = \frac{5}{8}$

B. $\frac{\boxed{}}{8} + \frac{\boxed{}}{8} = \frac{5}{8}$

$40 \div 4 =$

What is the value of the missing angle?

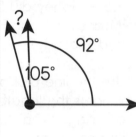

Day 2

Use the line plot below.

How many pieces of string are $4\frac{2}{4}$ inches?

Use the line plot below.

What is the difference in length between the longest and the shortest pieces of string.

Length of String in Inches

$3 \quad 3\frac{1}{4} \quad 3\frac{2}{4} \quad 3\frac{3}{4} \quad 4 \quad 4\frac{1}{4} \quad 4\frac{2}{4} \quad 4\frac{3}{4} \quad 5$

Day 3

Complete the table.

kg	g
1	1,000
2	
3	
4	
5	
6	
7	

$\frac{5}{10} + \frac{9}{100} = \frac{\boxed{}}{100}$

Draw the lines of symmetry on the flower.

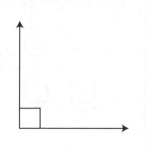

What kind of angle is shown?

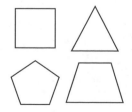

Day 4

Anna babysits 4 Saturdays in a row. Each Saturday, she earns $10.75. How much money does Anna earn in all 4 Saturdays combined?

If $\frac{4}{5} = 4 \times (\frac{1}{5})$, then

$\frac{4}{22} = \boxed{} \times (\frac{\boxed{}}{\boxed{}})$.

Write the decimal.

$\frac{36}{100} = $ _____

Color the shapes that have perpendicular or parallel sides.

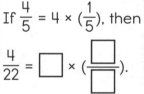

Name_____

1. Measure the angle.

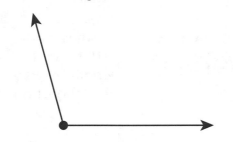

2. What is the value of the missing angle?

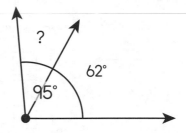

3. 12 kilograms = _____ grams

4. Samantha went out to eat with her friends on Monday, Tuesday, Wednesday, and Friday. She spent $5.65 on Monday, $7.50 on Tuesday, $9.75 on Wednesday, and $5.95 on Friday. How much more money did Samantha spend on Wednesday and Friday than on Monday and Tuesday?

5. Use the line plot below. How many pieces of string were measured?

6. Use the line plot below. What is the length of the shortest piece of string? What is the length of the longest piece of string?

Lengths of String in Inches

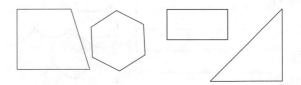

7. Draw a right angle.

8. Color the shapes that have perpendicular or parallel sides.

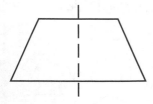

9. Circle the figure that shows a line of symmetry.

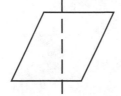

10. Decompose $\frac{8}{12}$ in two ways.

A. $\frac{\square}{2} + \frac{\square}{2} = \frac{8}{12}$

B. $\frac{\square}{2} + \frac{\square}{2} = \frac{8}{12}$

4.NF.3, 4.MD.1, 4.MD.2, 4.MD.4, 4.MD.5, 4.MD.6, 4.MD.7, 4.G.1, 4.G.2, 4.G.3   CD-104593 • © Carson-Dellosa

Name_____

Day 1

Spencer saves $2,458. He wants to invest $\frac{1}{2}$ of the money and put the rest in his savings account. How much money will Spencer invest?

Write <, >, or = to make the statement true.

0.72 ◯ 0.7

$2 \times \frac{8}{10} =$

Draw an acute angle.

Day 2

Measure the angle.

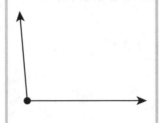

Write the equation.

Maria is 8 years old. Her mom is 4 times as old as Maria is. How old is Maria's mom?

Nikki's Italian Restaurant put $\frac{1}{4}$ of a gallon of oil in one batch of salad dressing. How many gallons of oil would be used in 4 batches of salad dressing?

Color the shapes that have obtuse angles.

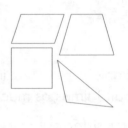

Day 3

Draw the lines of symmetry on the scissors.

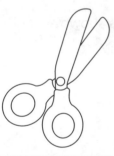

Round 65,567 to the nearest ten thousand.

Start at 901. Create a pattern that adds 112 to each number. Stop when you have 5 numbers.

What is the measure of the complete angle?

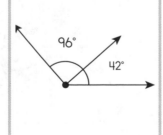

96°   42°

Day 4

Complete the table.

lbs.	oz.
1	16
2	
3	
4	
5	
6	
7	

$1,764 \div 9 =$

$23,456 - 19,001 =$

Lamar's milk shake recipe calls for $\frac{3}{10}$ of a scoop of ice cream. Tony's recipe calls for $\frac{8}{10}$ of a scoop of ice cream. How much more ice cream does Tony's milk shake call for than Lamar's?

75

Name_____

1. Write <, >, or = to make the statement true.

0.29 ◯ 0.39

2. Write the equation.

Luke has 7 marbles. His older brother has 7 times as many marbles as Luke. How many marbles does his older brother have?

3.

$4 \times \dfrac{3}{6} =$

4. 21 pounds = _____ ounces

5. Danielle put $582 in the bank. Her brother put 3 times as much money in the bank. Her sister put $\dfrac{1}{3}$ as much money in the bank. How much money combined did Danielle's brother and sister put in the bank?

6. Measure the angle.

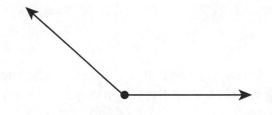

7. What is the measure of the complete angle?

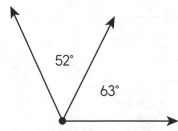

8. What kind of angle is shown?

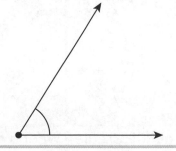

9. Color the shapes that have acute angles.

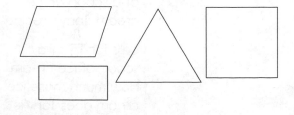

10. Draw the lines of symmetry on the snowflake.

 4.OA.1, 4.NF.4, 4.NF.7, 4.MD.1, 4.MD.2, 4.MD.5, 4.MD.6, 4.MD.7, 4.G.1, 4.G.2, 4.G.3   CD-104593 • © Carson-Dellosa

Name_____

Day 1

What kind of angle is shown?

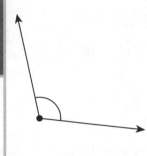

Draw the lines of symmetry on the tree.

Day 2

What is the measure of the complete angle?

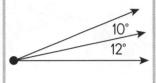

Zoe was collecting marbles. She got 10 marbles from the store and 5 from her mom. Zoe's teacher gave her 18 marbles. Zoe gave 12 marbles to her friend Xia. How many marbles does Zoe have left?

Round 234,675 to the nearest ten.

Complete the table.

L	mL
1	1,000
2	
3	
4	
5	
6	
7	

$985 \div 8 =$

Jasper needs 180 inches of string for his project. How many yards should he buy?

Day 3

Measure the angle.

Write the number in word form.

560,654

Day 4

Use the line plot below.

How many sticks measure $8\frac{4}{8}$ inches?

Use the line plot below.

What is the difference between the longest stick measured and the shortest stick measured?

$1,296 - 456 =$

Draw a parallelogram with exactly one right angle.

Lengths of Sticks in Inches

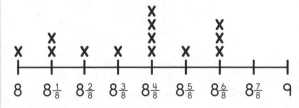

Name_____

1. Draw an obtuse angle.

2. Draw an isosceles right triangle.

3. Draw the lines of symmetry on the leaf.

4. Ty bought some stamps at the post office. Some of the stamps had flower designs, some had books, and some had flags. Ty bought 19 flower stamps. He bought 12 more book stamps than flower stamps and 20 fewer flag stamps than book stamps. How many stamps did Ty buy in all?

5. 30 liters = _____ milliliters

6. The toy racetrack is 60 inches long. How many feet is the toy racetrack?

7. Use the line plot below.

   How many sticks measured $9\frac{2}{8}$ inches?

8. Use the line plot below.

   How many sticks measured $9\frac{5}{8}$ inches and $9\frac{7}{8}$ inches?

Lengths of Sticks in Inches

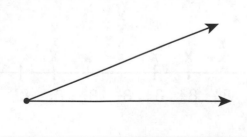

9. Measure the angle.

10. What is the measure of the complete angle?

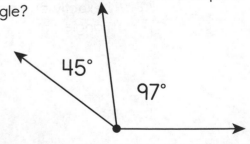

45°

97°

 4.OA.3, 4.MD.1, 4.MD.2, 4.MD.4, 4.MD.5, 4.MD.6, 4.MD.7, 4.G.1, 4.G.3   CD-104593 • © Carson-Dellosa

Name_____

Day 1

$3\frac{4}{8} + 1\frac{2}{8} =$

Draw a straight angle.

Which word describes the triangle?

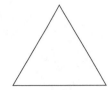

A. equilateral
B. isosceles
C. scalene

Day 2

$4\frac{5}{6} - 3\frac{1}{6} =$

Measure the angle.

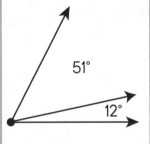

Virginia sold pizzas yesterday. Of the pizzas she sold, $\frac{2}{6}$ of them were large, and $\frac{4}{6}$ of them were extra large. What fraction of the pizzas sold were large or extra large?

If $\frac{4}{5} = 4 \times (\frac{1}{5})$,

then

$\frac{8}{10} = \boxed{} \times (\dfrac{\boxed{}}{\boxed{}})$.

Complete the table.

hr.	min.
1	60
2	
3	
4	
5	
6	
7	

Day 3

Ava and Becca are collecting canned goods.

Ava collected $\frac{3}{4}$ of a box of canned goods. If Becca collected 5 times as much as Ava, how much did Becca collect?

What is the measure of the complete angle?

51°

12°

Draw the lines of symmetry on the vase.

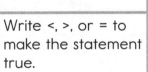

Day 4

$\dfrac{\boxed{}}{10} = \dfrac{60}{100}$

Is every square a quadrilateral?

Why or why not?

Write the decimal.

$\frac{56}{100} =$ _____

Write <, >, or = to make the statement true.

$\frac{4}{10} \bigcirc \frac{1}{8}$

Braden needs 16 quarts of punch for a party. How many gallons of punch does Braden need to buy?

Name_____

1. Which word describes the triangle?

   A. equilateral
   B. isosceles
   C. scalene

2. Is every trapezoid a parallelogram? Why or why not?

3. Draw the lines of symmetry on the butterfly.

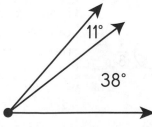

4. $1\frac{2}{8} + 5\frac{1}{8} =$

5. If $\frac{4}{5} = 4 \times (\frac{1}{5})$, then $\frac{4}{8} = \boxed{} \times (\frac{\boxed{}}{\boxed{}})$.

6. 12 hours = _____ minutes

7. Melissa needs 3 gallons of soup for her party. The restaurant packages the soup in quart bottles. How many bottles does she have to pick up?

8. Measure the angle.

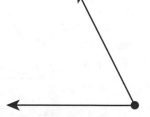

9. What is the measure of the complete angle?

11°
38°

10. What kind of angle is shown?

4.NF.3, 4.NF.4, 4.MD.1, 4.MD.2, 4.MD.5, 4.MD.6, 4.MD.7, 4.G.2, 4.G.3 CD-104593 • © Carson-Dellosa

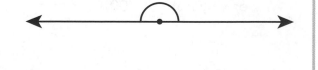

Name_____

Day 1

What is the value of the missing angle?

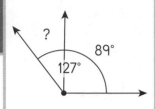

? 89° 127°

List the factors of 87.

Is this number prime or composite?

Day 2

Use the line plot below.

How many total cups of sugar were used to make cookies?

Use the line plot below.

How many times was $6\frac{1}{2}$ cups used in a recipe?

$\frac{2}{5} + \frac{2}{5} =$

Mrs. Lopez wanted to give 20 students calculators. Each calculator weighed 16 ounces. If Mrs. Lopez gave each student a calculator, how many pounds did the calculators weigh in all?

Cups of Sugar Used in Cookies

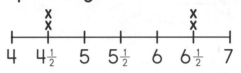

4    $4\frac{1}{2}$ 5 $5\frac{1}{2}$ 6 $6\frac{1}{2}$ 7

Day 3

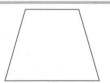

How many of each angle is in this shape?
acute _____
obtuse _____
right _____

$\frac{11}{12} - \frac{7}{12} =$

Day 4

Measure the angle.

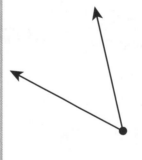

Draw the lines of symmetry on the hockey stick.

Determine the 30th figure in the pattern.

min.	sec.
1	60
2	
3	
4	
5	
6	
7	
8	

$4,562 \div 7 =$

Name this triangle (both names).

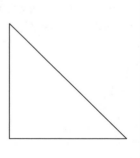

Name_____

1. Measure the angle.

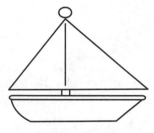

2. What is the value of the missing angle?

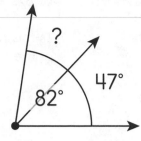

82° 47° ?

3.

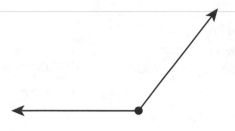

How many of each angle is in this shape?
acute _____
obtuse _____
right _____

4. Name this triangle (both names).

5. Draw the lines of symmetry on the boat.

6. $\frac{7}{8} - \frac{3}{8} =$

7. 45 minutes = _____ seconds

8. Two boxes of gold weigh 4 pounds 8 ounces. Each pound is worth $400. How much are the boxes of gold worth?

9. Use the line plot below.
How many total cups of flour were used to make cakes?

10. Use the line plot below.
What is the difference between the largest amount of flour used and the smallest amount of flour used?

Cups of Flour Used in Cakes

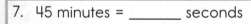

x x x x x x x

8 $8\frac{1}{2}$ 9 $9\frac{1}{2}$ 10 $10\frac{1}{2}$ 11

 4.NF.3, 4.MD.1, 4.MD.2, 4.MD.4, 4.MD.6, 4.MD.7, 4.G.1, 4.G.2, 4.G.3   CD-104593 • © Carson-Dellosa

Name_____

Day 1

Which word describes the triangle?

A. equilateral
B. isosceles
C. scalene

4,345 × 6 =

Day 2

What is the value of the missing angle?

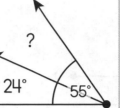

78,765 – 76,898 =

Write the number in word form.

144,657

Measure the angle.

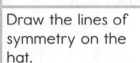

12 × 47 =

Draw the lines of symmetry on the hat.

Day 3

Circle the pentagon with parallel and perpendicular sides.

Write <, >, or = to make the statement true.

678,987 ◯ 675,897

4,893 ÷ 3 =

Day 4

Write <, >, or = to make the statement true.

$\frac{1}{8}$ ◯ $\frac{1}{4}$

Decompose $\frac{6}{10}$ in two ways.

A. $\frac{\square}{10} + \frac{\square}{10} = \frac{6}{10}$

B. $\frac{\square}{10} + \frac{\square}{10} = \frac{6}{10}$

Gary ran 14 yards on Tuesday and 34 yards on Wednesday. On Thursday, he ran 9 yards less than he ran on Wednesday. How many feet did Gary run altogether?

$7\frac{5}{8} - 6\frac{3}{8} =$

4 kilometers = _____ centimeters

Name_____

1. What is the value of the missing angle?

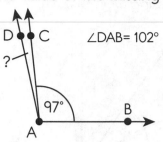

∠DAB= 102°

97°

2. Which word describes the triangle?

A. equilateral
B. isosceles
C. scalene

3. How many pairs of parallel sides does this figure have?

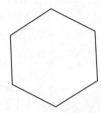

4. Draw the lines of symmetry.

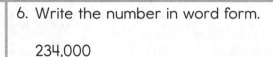

5. 2,456 × 7 =

6. Write the number in word form.

234,000

7. 4,332 ÷ 9 =

8. 8 kilometers = _____ centimeters

9. Erin ran 2 kilometers. Donna ran 3 kilometers. Reba ran 3 times as many kilometers as Donna. How many meters did Erin, Donna, and Reba run altogether?

10. Measure the angle.

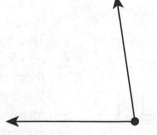

Name_____

Day 1

3 hours = _____ seconds

$5 \times \frac{2}{12} =$

Draw the lines of symmetry.

What is the measure of the complete angle?

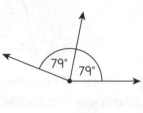

Day 2

Mr. Ahmed has 9 water heaters for his apartment buildings. Each heater weighs 32 kilograms. How many grams do all 9 water heaters weigh together?

Write the decimal.

$\frac{85}{100} =$ _____

$\frac{6}{10} = \frac{\square}{100}$

Which word describes the triangle?

A. right
B. acute
C. obtuse

Day 3

Use the line plot below.

What is the difference between the longest distance run and the shortest distance run?

Use the line plot below.

If you added all of the distances together, what would be the total distance run?

Miles Run

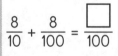

Day 4

$\frac{8}{10} + \frac{8}{100} = \frac{\square}{100}$

Measure the angle.

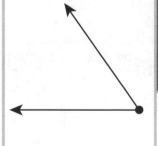

Jordan drew a shape. The shape had 3 unequal angles. What shape could Jordan have drawn?

$50,000 \div 5,000 =$

Name_____

---

1. Use the line plot below.
   What is the difference between the longest distance run and the shortest distance run?

2. Use the line plot below.
   If you added all of the distances together, what would be the total distance run?

Kilometers Run

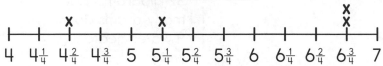

$4 \quad 4\frac{1}{4} \quad 4\frac{2}{4} \quad 4\frac{3}{4} \quad 5 \quad 5\frac{1}{4} \quad 5\frac{2}{4} \quad 5\frac{3}{4} \quad 6 \quad 6\frac{1}{4} \quad 6\frac{2}{4} \quad 6\frac{3}{4} \quad 7$

---

3. Measure the angle.

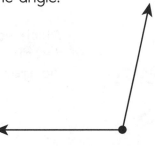

4. What is the measure of the complete angle?

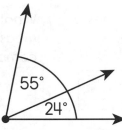

---

5. Which word describes the triangle?

   A. right
   B. acute
   C. obtuse

6. Norris cut a shape out of a sheet of paper. The shape had 4 sides, with opposite sides parallel. What shape could Norris have?
   A. hexagon
   B. parallelogram
   C. equilateral triangle

---

7. Draw the lines of symmetry.

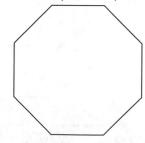

8. $8 \times \dfrac{7}{10} =$

---

9. 9 hours = _____ seconds

10. A serving of chicken has 18 grams of protein. The same size serving of fish has 25 grams of protein. How many more grams of protein does the fish have? How many more grams of protein are needed in the fish to equal a kilogram of protein?

 4.NF.4, 4.MD.1, 4.MD.2, 4.MD.4, 4.MD.6, 4.MD.7, 4.G.1, 4.G.2, 4.G.3 CD-104593 • © Carson-Dellosa

Name_____

Day 1

Write <, >, or = to make the statement true.

0.85 ◯ 0.74

If $\frac{4}{5} = 4 \times (\frac{1}{5})$, then

$\frac{3}{5} = $ ___ $\times (\frac{\Box}{\Box})$.

Day 2

7 hours = _____ seconds

A cafeteria has 23 tables. If 15 students can sit at each table, how many students can eat in the cafeteria at the same time?

The beaver walked $6\frac{4}{8}$ yards. The cat walked $2\frac{4}{8}$ yards. How many total inches did the beaver and the cat walk?

Round 543,456 to the nearest thousand.

$\frac{8}{12} - \frac{7}{12} = $

Circle the words that describe the shape.

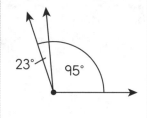

trapezoid
rhombus
quadrilateral
rectangle

Day 3

Blaine uses $\frac{7}{12}$ of a cup of flour in his cookies. Avery uses $\frac{4}{12}$ of a cup of flour in her cookies. How much more flour does Blaine use than Avery?

What is the measure of the complete angle?

23°   95°

Day 4

Monica uses $\frac{1}{3}$ of a pint of hair gel in her hair every day. How much gel does she use in 4 days?

Measure the angle.

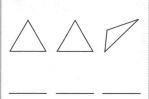

Draw the lines of symmetry.

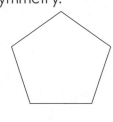

79,004 – 34,764 =

Label each triangle.
A. equilateral
B. isosceles
C. scalene

△ △ ◁

____ ____ ____

Write <, >, or = to make the statement true.

456,347 ◯ 356,764

Name_____

1. Cole walked $2\frac{1}{2}$ kilometers on Monday. Isabella walked twice as many kilometers as Cole. How many meters did Cole and Isabella walk altogether?

2. Measure the angle.

3. What is the measure of the complete angle?

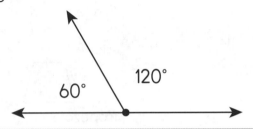

120°

60°

4. Label each triangle.
   A. right
   B. acute
   C. obtuse

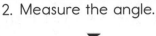

_____   _____   _____

5. Circle the words that describe the shape.

   rhombus
   quadrilateral
   parallelogram
   hexagon

6. Draw the lines of symmetry on the heart.

7. Write <, >, or = to make the statement true.

   0.9 ◯ 0.90

8. If $\frac{4}{5}$ = 4 × ($\frac{1}{5}$), then $\frac{9}{10}$ = ☐ × ($\frac{☐}{☐}$).

9. The Hat Hut has a selection of 4,578 hats. An equal number of cowboy hats, sun hats, and baseball hats are for sale. How many baseball hats are for sale at the Hat Hut?

10. 12 hours = _____ seconds

 4.OA.2, 4.NF.4, 4.NF.7, 4.MD.1, 4.MD.2, 4.MD.6, 4.MD.7, 4.G.1, 4.G.2, 4.G.3   CD-104593 • © Carson-Dellosa

Page 9

Day 1: 649; 3:30; Check students' answers; Check students' estimates; **Day 2:** 5,579; 50 books; 10, 12, 14; 1, 2, 4, composite; **Day 3:** 100,087; 300, 600, 300; 443; 1, 2, 4, 8, 16; **Day 4:** 65,303; 20 students; 97 pages; 10

Page 10

1. 6,551; 2. 4,868; 3. 50,000 + 9,000 + 6; 4. Check students' estimates; 5. 10; 6. 1, 2, 3, 6, composite; 7. 3, 9, 27, 81, 243; 8. 200, 100, 300; 9. Check students' answers; 10. 16, 18, 20

Page 11

Day 1: 632,770; C; 24 peanuts; 10; **Day 2:** Check students' estimates; 7, 12, 20; 132; 1, 7, prime; **Day 3:** 14,438; 6:10; 54; 2, 5, 11, 23, 47; **Day 4:** 67,134; 96 cents; pentagon; 50,000

Page 12

1. 44,000; 2. 400,002; 3. 10; 4. 1, 2, 5, 10, composite; 5. 5, 8, 11, 14, 17; 6. $9,007; 7. 9,800; 8. 67, 57, 62; 9. 3:15; 10. square

Page 13

Day 1: >; 100, 120, 140; 110; 1, 2, 3, 4, 6, 12, composite; **Day 2:** 600,008; 3 × 3 = 9; 965; 125, 119, 113, 107, 101; **Day 3:** 7,308; 5 × 3 = 15; 206 pages; 10; **Day 4:** 16,000; 59, 52; 18, 18, 16; >

Page 14

1. >; 2. 3,936; 3. 51,263; 4. 45,700; 5. 10; 6. 500, 496, 492, 488, 484; 7. 1, 3, 9, composite; 8. 6, 16, 4; 9. 4 × 2 = 8; 10. 25 photos

Page 15

Day 1: 1,496,772; 8, 4, 8; B; 180,000; **Day 2:** <; 12 feet; $4; 10; **Day 3:** 7,591; sunny; 860; 15 buds; **Day 4:** 363; 3 × 5 = 15; 60, 90, 120; 1, 11, prime

Page 16

1. 75,317; 2. 18 acorns; 3. 1, 2, 4, 7, 14, 28, composite; 4. 25,271; 5. 81,290; 6. 10; 7. 276; 8. C; 9. $4; 10. 5, 5, 8

Page 17

Day 1: 32,422; <; 8, 4, 4; ◯; **Day 2:** 53,859; 12; 55 arms; 10; **Day 3:** 713,923; 4, 6, 15; 15, 5, 24; 600,000; **Day 4:** <; 10; Check students' answers; 1, 2, 4, 11, 22, 44, composite

Page 18

1. 1, 5, 7, 35, composite; 2. ☆; 3. 140,687; 4. 88,000; 5. 9,631; 6. 5,067; 7. 10; 8. Check students' answers; 9. <; 10. 45, 7, 4

Page 19

Day 1: ⬠; 54 miles; <; 10; **Day 2:** 300,000 + 30,000 + 9,000 + 6; 300; 40, 360, 60; 1, 19, prime; **Day 3:** 13,122; 77, 73, 69; No; $\frac{1}{2}$ and $\frac{4}{8}$; **Day 4:** 7,700; Check students' answers; $14; 222

Page 20

1. 679; 2. 41,984; 3. 10; 4. 713,920; 5. ◯; 6. 1, 2, 3, 5, 6, 10, 15, 30, composite; 7. 926,186; 8. 3, 7, 72; 9. No; 10. Yes

Page 21

Day 1: 904,503; Yes; 24 inches; 10;
Day 2: 3,065; $\frac{2}{8}$; 8:50; 30,000; **Day 3:** 40,890; 820; 40 legs; 22 marbles; **Day 4:** 1, 3, 13, 39, composite; 585, 575, 565; $7\frac{1}{4}$ inches; >

Page 22

1. =; 2. 578,999; 3. 10 pencils; 4. 10; 5. 1, 17, prime; 6. 400,000; 7. 14,009; 8. 30,000 + 8,000 + 500 + 20 + 5; 9. $9\frac{1}{2}$ inches; 10. 9:50

Page 23

Day 1: 1, 2, 7, 14, composite; <, <, =; 154, 157, 160; >; **Day 2:** 5, 13, 37, 109, 325; 20 pictures; Check students' answers; 95,000; **Day 3:** 10; 2 trees; 150 tickets; 57,435; **Day 4:** 40,000 + 1,000 + 900 + 80 + 4; 62; two hundred twelve; 9,097

Page 24

1. 110,539; 2. 693,726; 3. 11,910; 4. 66,418; 5. 10; 6. 4, 7, 13, 25, 49; 7. 1, 2, 3, 4, 6, 8, 12, 24, composite; 8. Check students' work; 9. 15 students; 10. 212, 215, 218

Page 25

Day 1: 632,795; 9, 42, 9; 489; 1, 2, 3, 4, 6, 9, 12, 18, 36, composite; **Day 2:** 38,908; 340; $16;

; **Day 3:** <; 350, 210, 450; 6 × 9 = 54 or 9 × 6 = 54; 10; **Day 4:** 95,175; 8 golf clubs; 5 × 5 = 25, 25 × 4 = 100; $13,852

Page 26

1. Check students' estimates; 2. ; 3. 10; 4. 1, 23, prime; 5. 2,000 + 100 + 20 + 4; 6. =; 7. 544; 8. 619,158; 9. 3, 6, 16; 10. 3 buckets

Page 27

Day 1: 900,000; 5:03; 974; 29 spots;
Day 2: 785,856; D; 8, 2, 2; 87,478;
Day 3: 78,999; Check students' answers; <; <;
Day 4: 1, 2, 4, 5, 10, 20, composite; 20 cm; yes; 10

Page 28

1. 10; 2. 1, 3, 11, 33, composite; 3. 27,703; 4. 55,751; 5. 15 stickers; 6. 17,000; 7. 200,000 + 50,000 + 9,000 + 300 + 40 + 1; 8. <; 9. Check students' answers; 10. A

Page 29

Day 1: 3 × 4 = 12; 26,100; >; 210; **Day 2:** 1,800 miles; 10, 100, 1,000, 10,000, 100,000; 122,631; 6 cm; **Day 3:** 21 tourists; 1, 79, prime; 65,932; 70 square meters; **Day 4:** 7, 4, 5; 10; 37,890; 80

Page 30

1. 135 books; 2. 320; 3. 640,000; 4. 8 feet; 5. 5, 25, 125, 625, 3,125; 6. 7 × 6 = 42; 7. 8, 7, 12; 8. 1, 2, 3, 4, 6, 7, 12, 14, 21, 28, 42, 84, composite; 9. 20 square meters; 10. 27 photos

Page 31

Day 1: 20 feet; 827,677; 266; 192 students;
Day 2: $25 × 6 = $150; 10; 1, 2, 3, 4, 5,
6, 10, 12, 15, 20, 30, 60, composite; 410;
Day 3: 20 students; 125,169; 528; 7, 1, 2;
Day 4: 21 inches; 69,600; 439,000; 246

Page 32

1. 388; 2. 88 people; 3. 33 × 5 = 165; 4. 3, 2,
8; 5. 603; 6. 45 inches; 7. 32 centimeters;
8. 80,000 + 7,000 + 400 + 70 + 8; 9. 10; 10. 192
times

Page 33

Day 1: 93; 258 bulbs; 213,500; 57 feet;
Day 2: 6,412; 19 inches; 10; 7 inches;
Day 3: 928; 265,276; 17,433; 7 × 9 = 63;
Day 4: 49; 963; 1, 59, prime; 210 coupons

Page 34

1. 48 inches; 2. 36 centimeters; 3. 92; 4. 89,245;
5. 270 minutes; 6. 21 × 4 = 84; 7. 740,000;
8. 1,675; 9. 156 inches; 10. 15 hours, 900 minutes

Page 35

Day 1: 3,160 people; 5 feet; 980,507; 4,644;
Day 2: 60 apples; 4, 19, 79, 319, 1,279; 54,680;
35 r6; **Day 3:** 32 × 9 = 288 pretzel rods; >;
70,000 + 6,000 + 700 + 80 + 9; 217;
Day 4: 294; 34,989; 10; 2 feet

Page 36

1. 4 feet; 2. 5,751; 3. 1,134; 4. 10 feet; 5. 2, 12, 42,
132, 402; 6. 33,667; 7. 92 r2; 8. 144 biscuits;
9. 18 × 6 = 108; 10. 55,700

Page 37

Day 1: 30,006; $51 × 5 = $255; 334,608; 29
meters; **Day 2:** 44,335; 5,892; 1, 2, 4, 17, 34,
68, composite; 12 inches; **Day 3:** 81; 248,700;
1,000, 992, 984, 976, 968; 40 boxes; **Day 4:** 129;
66,728; 186,755; 307 lessons

Page 38

1. 32,912; 2. 10 inches; 3. 9 miles; 4. 342,608;
5. 4 × 8 = 32; 6. 16; 7. 56 inches; 8. 103,496;
9. 1, 67, prime; 10. 2,337 tickets

Page 39

Day 1: 1,547; 193,058; 9 yards; 20 × 7 = 140;
Day 2: 115 r1; 229,494; 462,150; 1,724 ribbons;
Day 3: 92, 105, 118, 131, 144; 10; 6,160; 15;
Day 4: fifty thousand three hundred twenty-
eight; 11 centimeters; 35; 912

Page 40

1. 6,960; 2. 13 r1; 3. 5 feet; 4. 256 stickers;
5. 1,332 people; 6. 45,525; 7. 5 feet; 8. 10; 9.
five hundred three thousand two hundred
eight; 10. 8 × 9 = 72

Page 41

Day 1: 44 people; 759,026; 700,000 + 20,000 + 1,000 + 900 + 4; 51 millimeters; **Day 2:** 5,678 × 2 = 11,356; 190 cans; 10; 501; **Day 3:** 18 seashells; 200,000; ⬡; 4,895; **Day 4:** 345 centimeters; <; 1, 3, 5, 15, 25, 75, composite; 8,008

Page 42

1. 2,006; 2. 912 yards; 3. 72 tickets; 4. 3,360; 5. 85,569; 6. 740,000; 7. 3,465 feet; 8. 19,701; 9. 22 feet; 10. 33 × 5 = 165

Page 43

Day 1: 2,112; 820,515; 234 × 4 = 936; 19 feet; **Day 2:** 8,492; 248,000; <; 12 feet; **Day 3:** 91; 977,319; 10; 294 hours; **Day 4:** 44 r4; 89,731; 12, 48, 192, 768, 3,072; 49 habitats

Page 44

1. 29 rooms; 2. 192; 3. 43,016; 4. 600 miles; 5. 25 yards; 6. 329,200; 7. 375,050; 8. 132 × 5 = 660; 9. 4,089; 10. 13 feet

Page 45

Day 1: 789; 1, 61, prime; 241,460; 144 inches; **Day 2:** 1,026; 7, 49, 343, 2,401, 16,807; 926,347; 11 fish; **Day 3:** 10; 15,618; 61 r1; 21 outfits; **Day 4:** 17 feet; eight hundred forty-one thousand five hundred four; 2,700; 16 × 2 = 192

Page 46

1. 40 cards; 2. 1, 2, 5, 7, 10, 14, 35, 70, composite; 3. 6 inches; 4. 912; 5. 158, 166, 174, 182, 190; 6. 7 boxes, $1; 7. 362 r3; 8. 16 feet; 9. 125 × 2 = 250; 10. 997,259

Page 47

Day 1: $62; 968; 128,688; 5 feet; **Day 2:** $2; 900; 10; >; **Day 3:** 850 × 6 = 5,100; 20,965; 460,000; 225; **Day 4:** 112 inches; 925 r4; 722,170; 114,258

Page 48

1. $4; 2. 989; 3. 680; 4. 43 × 8 = 344; 5. 37 meters; 6. 10; 7. <; 8. 104 crafts; 9. 7 inches; 10. 462

Page 49

Day 1: >; 9 × 7 = 63; 4, 20, 100, 500, 2,500; $\frac{4}{4}$ = 1 hour; **Day 2:** $\frac{4}{5}$; 1,968 bottles; 10; 40; **Day 3:** 1, 1, and 1; 38 bags, 23 bags; >; 0.5; **Day 4:** $5\frac{2}{3}$; 1, 2, 19, 38, composite; eighty-three thousand six hundred two; 19

Page 50

1. >; 2. $\frac{2}{3}$; 3. 1, 1, 1, 1, and 1, 1; 4. $4\frac{3}{5}$; 5. $\frac{3}{4}$ of an hour; 6. 50; 7. 0.8; 8. 45; 9. 8 × 8 = 64; 10. 736 boxes

Page 51

Day 1: 540,000; 192; $\frac{7}{12}$ of a mile; <; **Day 2:** 19,222; 56 meters; 80; $\frac{4}{6}$; **Day 3:** 2,043; 172 r2; 77; 1, 1, and 2; **Day 4:** 1,232; 16 meters; 0.33; $5\frac{8}{8}$ or 6

Page 52

1. 687,160; 2. 18,101; 3. 0.87; 4. 48; 5. 90; 6. $\frac{9}{10}$ of a mile; 7. $5\frac{6}{5} = 6\frac{1}{5}$; 8. 1, 1, 1, and 2; 9. $\frac{3}{7}$; 10. =

Page 53

Day 1: $14\frac{4}{8}$; 1, 2, 17, 34; composite; ☆; 52;
Day 2: 1, 1, and 1; 27 toothbrushes; 10; 0.64;
Day 3: $\frac{2}{4}$; 75 CDs; 89,980; 70; **Day 4:** =; 2 × 12 = 24; 15,000; $\frac{5}{4} = 1\frac{1}{4}$ cups

Page 54

1. 85 bars, 340 bars; 2. 1, 2, 4, 8, 16, composite;
3. $\frac{83}{100}$; 4. 0.49; 5. <; 6. $\frac{5}{12}$; 7. 4, 5; 8. $4\frac{1}{2}$;
9. $\frac{6}{8} = \frac{3}{4}$; 10. 60

Page 55

Day 1: $5\frac{8}{6} = 6\frac{1}{3}$; 52,665; $\frac{5}{6}$; 33; **Day 2:** $\frac{5}{6}$; 408;
$\frac{2}{12} = \frac{1}{6}$; 0.7; **Day 3:** =; 57; 0.32; $\frac{3}{3}$ = 1 pizza;
Day 4: 3, 4; 9 feet; 29,256; 4

Page 56

1. 651; 2. =; 3. 301; 4. $\frac{6}{8} = \frac{3}{4}$; 5. 0.14; 6. 2, 1, 1;
7. 16; 8. $4\frac{1}{10}$; 9. 7; 10. $\frac{5}{6}$ of a pizza

Page 57

Day 1: 3,894 flags; 2; $\frac{8}{12} = \frac{2}{3}$; 125;
Day 2: 10,025; $\frac{9}{10}$ of the pie; >; 10; **Day 3:** 10,881;
$\frac{99}{100}$; $5\frac{6}{8} = 5\frac{3}{4}$; <; **Day 4:** 132 pounds; 0.54;
Check students' answers; 320,150

Page 58

1. $\frac{7}{12}$ of the bag; 2. 8; 3. $7\frac{16}{12} = 8\frac{1}{3}$; 4. 71;
5. Check students' answers; 6. 0.26; 7. $\frac{7}{8}$; 8. 45
books, 90 books; 9. >; 10. 10

Page 59

Day 1: 4 × $(\frac{1}{6})$; $\frac{1}{12}$; 1, 2, 3, 5, 6, 9, 10, 15, 18, 30,
45, 90, composite; <; **Day 2:** $\frac{6}{3}$ = 2; 5; 12 feet;
$\frac{2}{8} = \frac{1}{4}$; **Day 3:** $\frac{16}{3} = 5\frac{1}{3}$ pounds; 25; 41,201;
Check students' answers; **Day 4:** <; 0.06;
10 × 6 = 60 stickers; $2\frac{2}{3}$

Page 60

1. 6 × $(\frac{1}{10})$; 2. $\frac{8}{5} = 1\frac{3}{5}$; 3. $\frac{18}{5} = 3\frac{3}{5}$ cups; 4. >; 5. <;
6. $\frac{2}{8} = \frac{1}{4}$; 7. Check students' answers; 8. $\frac{2}{6} = \frac{1}{3}$; 9. $\frac{3}{8}$ of the pan; 10. 9

Page 61

Day 1: 0.68; $3\frac{2}{5}$; 5,604; >; **Day 2:** 2 × $(\frac{1}{8})$;
$\frac{2}{4} = \frac{1}{2}$ of the apple; 468; >; **Day 3:** $\frac{12}{5}$ or
$2\frac{2}{5}$; 20; 43 paper clips with 7 left over; $\frac{1}{6}$;
Day 4: $\frac{8}{12} = \frac{2}{3}$ of pizza; 68; 800,000 + 40,000
+ 3; Check students' answers.

Page 62

1. 30; 2. <; 3. $1\frac{4}{10}$; 4. $\frac{16}{6} = 2\frac{2}{3}$ cups; 5. Check
students' answers; 6. $\frac{9}{10}$; 7. $\frac{1}{3}$; 8. 2 × $(\frac{1}{4})$; 9. <;
10. 0.29

Page 63

Day 1: 7 × $(\frac{1}{3})$; $\frac{1}{4}$ of the orange; 4, 16, 64,
256, 1,024; <; **Day 2:** $\frac{27}{4} = 6\frac{3}{4}$; 0.4; 188,000;
$\frac{1}{6}$; **Day 3:** $\frac{28}{8} = 3\frac{1}{2}$ cups of oatmeal; 10; 25;
Check students' answers; **Day 4:** >; 47; 8 × 3 = 24 gems; $3\frac{2}{5}$

Page 64

1. <; 2. $\frac{4}{6} = \frac{2}{3}$; 3. <; 4. Check students' answers;
5. $\frac{28}{10} = 2\frac{4}{5}$ cups; 6. $1\frac{4}{8} = 1\frac{1}{2}$; 7. $\frac{8}{6} = 1\frac{1}{3}$;
8. $\frac{3}{5}$ of a bag; 9. $10 \times (\frac{1}{6})$; 10. 0.36

Page 65

Day 1: 7 tents; $\frac{1}{4}$ of a gallon; <; 0.28;
Day 2: 422,951; $5 \times (\frac{1}{12})$; $\frac{5}{10}$; 30; **Day 3:** 200,
400, 800, 1,600, 3,200; $\frac{6}{10} = \frac{3}{5}$; Check students'
answers; 64; **Day 4:** 139,660; $\frac{40}{8} = 5$ packages;
$2\frac{2}{12} = 2\frac{1}{6}$; =

Page 66

1. <; 2. $\frac{7}{8}$; 3. Check students' answers;
4. $4\frac{4}{10} = 4\frac{2}{5}$; 5. $\frac{6}{12} = \frac{1}{2}$ of a banana; 6. $7 \times (\frac{1}{8})$;
7. $\frac{15}{10} = 1\frac{1}{2}$; 8. $\frac{8}{4} = 2$ tablespoons; 9. =; 10. 39

Page 67

Day 1: >; 0.73; 588; $\frac{3}{8}$ of a bottle; **Day 2:** $\frac{3}{10}$;
3; 47 pieces; $6 \times (\frac{1}{6})$; **Day 3:** Check students'
answers; $\frac{94}{100}$; 300,000; $\frac{16}{8} = 2$; **Day 4:** $4\frac{4}{6} = 4\frac{2}{3}$;
<; 820, 850, 880, 910, 940; $\frac{18}{12} = 1\frac{1}{2}$ cups

Page 68

1. $\frac{6}{8} = \frac{3}{4}$; 2. $1\frac{2}{3}$; 3. $9 \times (\frac{1}{5})$; 4. $\frac{24}{4} = 6$
tablespoons; 5. >; 6. 0.95; 7. $\frac{7}{2} = 3\frac{1}{2}$;
8. $\frac{3}{6} = \frac{1}{2}$ of the potpie; 9. Check students'
answers; 10. =

Page 69

Day 1: 200, 300, 400, 500, 600, 700; $\rightleftarrows$;
538; 45°; **Day 2:** 90 minutes = $1\frac{1}{2}$ hours;
352,889; 258,608; Check students' answers;
Day 3: 2 inches; 5; **Day 4:** 79,008; 90°; Check
students' answers; $10

Page 70

1. 10,000; 2. 12:10; 3. $1\frac{1}{2}$ inches; 4. 4 books;
5. 45°; 6. 23°; 7. parallel lines; 8. Check
students' answers; 9. Students should have
drawn one line of symmetry; 10. 743,201

Page 71

Day 1: 350,007; Check students' answers; 175°;
21 books; **Day 2:** 2,000, 3,000, 4,000, 5,000,
6,000, 7,000; 12,000; 956; perpendicular lines;
Day 3: 5,610; Check students' answers; 70°; 41,
123, 369, 1,107; **Day 4:** 320 kilometers; 500,000;
$\frac{3}{4}$; $7\frac{6}{8} = 7\frac{3}{4}$

Page 72

1. 177 tables; 2. 15,000; 3. 15 kilometers, 22
hours and 30 minutes; 4. 500,000; 5. 1,278,
1,128, 978, 828, 678; 6. 30°; 7. 15°; 8. Check
students' answers; 9. Check students' answers;
10. Students should have drawn zero lines of
symmetry.

Page 73

Day 1: 32°; Check students' answers; 10; 13°; **Day 2:** 4; $1\frac{1}{4}$ inches; **Day 3:** 2,000, 3,000, 4,000, 5,000, 6,000, 7,000; Students should have drawn three lines of symmetry; 59; right angle; **Day 4:** $43; 4 × $(\frac{1}{22})$; 0.36; Check students' answers.

Page 74

1. 105°; 2. 33°; 3. 12,000; 4. $2.55; 5. 12 pieces; 6. $4\frac{1}{4}$ inches, 6 inches; 7. Check students' answers; 8. Check students' answers; 9. Check students' answers; 10. Check students' answers.

Page 75

Day 1: $1,229; >; $\frac{16}{10} = 1\frac{3}{5}$; Check students' answers; **Day 2:** 95°; 8 × 4 = 32; $\frac{4}{4} = 1$ gallon; Check students' answers; **Day 3:** Students should have drawn one line of symmetry; 70,000; 901, 1,013, 1,125, 1,237, 1,349; 138°; **Day 4:** 32, 48, 64, 80, 96, 112; 196; 4,455; $\frac{5}{10} = \frac{1}{2}$

Page 76

1. <; 2. 7 × 7 = 49; 3. $\frac{12}{6} = 2$; 4. 336; 5. $1,940; 6. 138°; 7. 115°; 8. acute angle; 9. Check students' answers; 10. Students should have drawn six lines of symmetry.

Page 77

Day 1: obtuse angle; Students should have drawn one line of symmetry; 234,680; 2,000, 3,000, 4,000, 5,000, 6,000; **Day 2:** 22°; 21; 123 r1; 5 yards; **Day 3:** 115°; five hundred sixty thousand six hundred fifty-four; 840; Check students' answers;
Day 4: 4; $\frac{6}{8} = \frac{3}{4}$ inches

Page 78

1. Check students' answers; 2. Check students' answers; 3. Students should have drawn one line of symmetry; 4. 61; 5. 30,000; 6. 5 feet; 7. 0; 8. 4; 9. 22°; 10. 142°

Page 79

Day 1: $4\frac{6}{8} = 4\frac{3}{4}$; Check students' answers; 142°; $\frac{6}{6} = 1$; **Day 2:** A; $1\frac{4}{6} = 1\frac{2}{3}$; 8 × $(\frac{1}{10})$; 120, 180, 240, 300, 360, 420; **Day 3:** $\frac{15}{4} = 3\frac{3}{4}$; 63°; Yes, because all quadrilaterals and all squares have 4 sides; 0.56; **Day 4:** Students should have drawn one line of symmetry; 6; >; 4 gallons

Page 80

1. B; 2. No, a right trapezoid only has one pair of parallel sides; 3. Students should have drawn one line of symmetry; 4. $6\frac{3}{8}$; 5. 4 × $(\frac{1}{8})$; 6. 720; 7. 12 quarts; 8. 63°; 9. 49°; 10. straight angle

Page 81

Day 1: 38°; 1, 3, 29, 87, composite; $\frac{4}{5}$; 20 pounds; **Day 2:** 22 cups, 2 times; **Day 3:** 2, 2, 0; $\frac{4}{12} = \frac{1}{3}$; ☆; 120, 180, 240, 300, 360, 420; **Day 4:** 49°; Students should have drawn zero lines of symmetry; 651 r5; isosceles, right triangle

Page 82

1. 127°; 2. 35°; 3. 2, 0, 1; 4. scalene, right triangle; 5. Students should have drawn zero lines of symmetry; 6. $\frac{4}{8} = \frac{1}{2}$; 7. 2,700; 8. $3,600; 9. $66\frac{1}{2}$ cups of flour; 10. 3 cups

Page 83

Day 1: C; 26,070; one hundred forty-four thousand six hundred fifty-seven; 13°; **Day 2:** 31°; 1,867; 564; Students should have drawn one line of symmetry; **Day 3:** Check students' answers; >; Check students' answers; 219 feet; **Day 4:** 1,631; <; $1\frac{2}{8} = 1\frac{1}{4}$; 400,000

Page 84

1. 5°; 2. C; 3. 3; 4. Students should have drawn two lines of symmetry; 5. 17,192; 6. two hundred thirty-four thousand; 7. 481 r3; 8. 800,000; 9. 14,000 meters; 10. 82°

Page 85

Day 1: 10,800; $\frac{10}{12} = \frac{5}{6}$; Students should have drawn two lines of symmetry; 158°; **Day 2:** 288,000; 0.85; 60; C; **Day 3:** 2 miles; $37\frac{1}{2}$ miles; **Day 4:** 88; 55°; scalene triangle; 10

Page 86

1. $2\frac{1}{4}$ kilometers; 2. $23\frac{1}{4}$ kilometers; 3. 102°; 4. 79°; 5. C; 6. B; 7. Students should have drawn eight lines of symmetry; 8. $\frac{56}{10} = 5\frac{3}{5}$; 9. 32,400; 10. 7 grams, 975 grams

Page 87

Day 1: >; 3 × ($\frac{1}{5}$); 324 inches; 543,000; **Day 2:** 25,200; 345; $\frac{1}{12}$; trapezoid, quadrilateral; **Day 3:** $\frac{1}{4}$ of a cup; 118°; Students should have drawn one line of symmetry; 44,240; **Day 4:** $\frac{4}{3} = 1\frac{1}{3}$ pints; 158°; Check students' answers; >

Page 88

1. 7,500 meters; 2. 27°; 3. 180°; 4. Check students' answers; 5. rhombus, parallelogram; 6. Students should have drawn one line of symmetry; 7. =; 8. 9 × ($\frac{1}{10}$); 9. 1,526; 10. 43,200